Advanced Pressure Point Grappling

by George A. Dillman with Chris Thomas

TUITÉ

The Dillman Method of Instant Self-Defense

A George Dillman Karate International Book

First published in 1995 by:
George Dillman Karate International
251 Mt. View Rd. (Grill)
Reading, PA 19607
U.S.A.

A NOTE TO THE READER

The ideas, techniques, and beliefs expressed in this book are the result of years of study and practice. The knowledge contained within is a synthesis of training which was obtained from martial arts experts over a period of three decades.

This book is written as a means of preserving a vital, historical aspect of the martial arts. George Dillman Karate International Publishers and the authors make no representation, warranty, or guarantee that the techniques described and illustrated in this book will be effective or safe in any self-defense situation or otherwise. You may be injured if you apply or train in the techniques offered within. We therefore suggest you use restraint when practicing all techniques contained within this book, and practice only under the supervision of a qualified instructor. The George Dillman Karate International Publishers and the authors are in no way responsible for any injuries that may result. Some self-defense techniques illustrated within may not be justified in some circumstances under applicable federal, state, or local law. Neither George Dillman Karate International Publishers nor the authors make any representation or warranty regarding the appropriateness of any technique mentioned in this book.

Printed in the United States of America.

Ben Godbold (275 lbs.) is knocked out on triple warmer points during an advanced seminar at Jacksonville, FL. (Oct. 1993) by George A. Dillman.

Dedications

This book is dedicated to my good friends and instructors--Professor Wally Jay, without whose "small circle" my techniques would be incomplete; Professor Remy Presas, without whose "flow" my techniques would not have crossed the boundaries of style and art form; and Grandmaster Seiyu Oyata whose knowledge rekindled my search for the true meanings of kata. Thank you for sharing this experience.

—George Dillman

This work is dedicated to my family, Wendy, Josh and April, and my instructors, Robert Fusaro, Steve Young, and George Dillman.

—Chris Thomas

ACKNOWLEDGEMENTS

We would like to gratefully acknowledge the many people who have made this book possible. Our thanks to Wendy Countryman for principal photography, Tom Countryman for artwork, and Willy Blumhoff Designs for layout.

Thanks to those who appear in the photos: Ed Lake, Bill Burch, Dave Poirier, Warren Williams, Wendy Countryman, Kim Dillman, Harvey Flesberg, and especially Adam Caswell, Josh Countryman, April Countryman, and Jason Poirier, the next generation of black belts and our hope for the future. And to Ron Richards for being in the cover photo.

Our deepest thanks to our teachers for showing us the way, and to our students who have encouraged us in it. We are also grateful to the many Dillman Karate International black belts around the world who, by their own research, are contributing daily to our understanding of the secrets of the art.

Photos on this page by: Kim Dillman.

▲ While in California doing a Black Belt Magazine cover shot (March 1995). The gang from DKI stopped by for the fantastic food at Rosy's Restaurant in Burbank.

George A. Dillman demonstrates a thumb lock on Kim McMenamin at his Buncrana, Ireland seminar. (April 1994) ▶

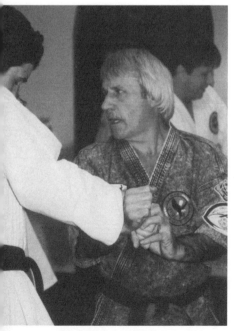

▲ Bob Golden "The Pitt Bull" shows a seminar participant a grappling technique using pressure points to stop the attacker. (Oct. 1993)

▲ George A. Dillman, taps out another knockout to a volunteer during a packed house Chicago area seminar.

▲ George A. Dillman catches a volunteer from a Chicago area seminar. (Oct. 1993)

All Photos by: Kim Dillman.
except bottom right by: Richard Paul, London England

◀ George A. Dillman uses pressure points to drop a seminar participant in London, England. (April 1994)

▲ Hail, Hail the gangs all here! Jacksonville, Florida seminar 1994. George Dillman, Bernice and Wally Jay gather with the Black Belts at Jack Hogan's house.

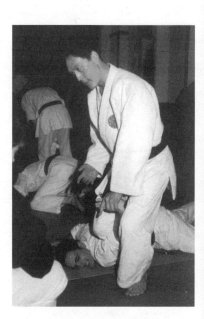

▲ Prof. Wally Jay and George A. Dillman just before they saw the "Black Bear" in the woods. (1994) Jacksonville, Florida.

▲ Leon Jay in London, England uses pressure points with his life-long grappling study.

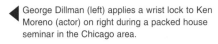

◀ George Dillman (left) applies a wrist lock to Ken Moreno (actor) on right during a packed house seminar in the Chicago area.

All photos on both pages by: Kim Dillman
except for Eileen Mejia knocking out husband (left page bottom r

(Standing left to right) Will Higginbotham, Michelle Balchaitis, Bernie Grundhoefer, Jack Hogan, Remy Presas, George Dillman, Wally Jay, Jim Corn, Dave Converse, Dave Wilson, Ian Waite (New Zealand representative). (Kneeling left to right) Dr. Chas Terry, Greg Dillon, Frank Monea (Australian representative), Mark Kline, Dr. Ralph Buschbacher, Bill Burch.

▲ George A. Dillman, knocks out Andrew Kluk at his Tae Kwon Do School in N.W. Chicago during a packed house "pressure point" seminar. (Oct. 1993)

Eileen Mejia knocks out her husband Kevin during a Chicago Area demonstration outdoors using Dillman Theory "pressure point" strikes. (photo: Betty Sexton) ▶

▲ The Dillman Karate International Team has traveled the world teaching and sharing the theory of pressure points… St. Augustine, Florida. (left to right) Clara and Jack Hogan, Will Higginbotham, Sandra Schlessman, George A. Dillman, Prof. Remy Presas and Charlie Dean, kneeling is Jim Corn.

▲ The party gang at Put-in-Bay Lake Erie Island, Ohio following a seminar. (left to right) Frank Annese, George Dillman, Mark Kline and Bill Burch

▲ Leon Jay and George Dillman at Winchester Cathedral, Winchester, England at the small version of the round table used by King Arthur.

▲ October 1993, Bill Burch got "Married" and the DKI Team pictured were best men: (left to right) Greg Dillon, Bill, George A. Dillman, Mark Kline, Bob Golden, Will Higginbotham, and kneeling is Jim Corn

▲ George A. Dillman demonstrates the pressure points to be used when kneeling or on the ground… Ed Lake is knocked out with a touch as Jack Hogan catches him.

▲ Ohio Seminar 1994 – over 100 attended…
(left to right) Frank Annese, Mark Kline,
George A. Dillman, Bill Burch and Tom Smith.

▼ 1985 – The Spectrum (Philadelphia, Pennsylvania). 17,000 people gave George A. Dillman and his team a standing ovation… As Dillman did his last "Ice Break" of 1,000 lbs. Watching this feat were Michael Jordan (Bulls vs. 76ers) Julius Irving and Charles Barkley. (Photo: H. James Clapp)

▲ George A. Dillman and Jack Hogan attempt to revive the KO'd Ed Lake.

This is healing? Bernice Jay ▶ works on the pressure points of Kim Dillman during a seminar break… (1994)

George A. Dillman knocks out Doug Arndt of California during a seminar in Terre Haute, Indiana (1993). ▶

▲ Bob "Pitt Bull" Golden looks on as student Dr. David Taylor taps out Dave Peterson.

▲ The Best Awards: Houston Texas (1993) over 300 attended Big 3 seminar - covered by Black Belt Magazine. (left to right) Charlie Dean, Wally Jay, Tom Muncy, Remy Presas, Rick Moneymaker, George Dillman and Randy Fuller.

▲ Ralph Lindquist and George A. Dillman (1980's) at the Northeast Open Karate Championships, Hamburg Fieldhouse, north of Reading, Pennsylvania.

TABLE OF CONTENTS

Ron Richards during a pressure point training workshop easily knocks out Glenn Davis from New Jersey (A student of Barry Black). (Here Ron combines the grappling or grabbing of Tuité and the striking of Kyusho-jitsu) 1994 photo.

HISTORY OF RYUKYU KEMPO

The art which we know as karate developed on the Ryukyu archipelago, a chain of islands between Japan and China. The largest of these islands is Okinawa, so the terms Ryukyu and Okinawa are used interchangeably. Because of its location, the Ryukyus became a meeting point for Japanese and Chinese culture.

By 1393, a Chinese economic and cultural mission was established in Okinawa. There, well-bred Okinawans learned to speak and read Chinese. They were also educated in Chinese governmental administration, and in many cases travelled to China for further study. In this way, Okinawans became familiar with Chinese culture, including the methods of Chinese boxing. Nowadays Chinese boxing is called "kung fu", but the original name is "chuan fa" ("fist method") which is pronounced "kempo" in the Okinawan dialect.

In 1507, circumstances arose which were particularly favorable to the development of kempo on Okinawa. At that time, the second king of Okinawa, Sho Shin-O, ended feudalism in the Ryukyu kingdom, and unified the islands. Part of Sho Shin-O's reforms was to outlaw the private ownership of weapons. In this setting, self-defense methods with a strong component of empty-hand fighting would, quite naturally, become highly favored. Since kempo is a fighting system based on empty-hand combat (even kempo's associated weapons systems are based on the empty-hand movements, unlike the Japanese fighting arts which developed empty-hand techniques based on weapon handling) it found a fertile ground in which to flourish.

In 1609, the Satsuma samurai clan of Japan invaded and subjugated Okinawa. While the Ryukyu monarchy continued to exist, it remained under the thumb of the Satsuma until the throne was abdicated in 1879 (at which time Okinawa officially became a part of Japan). As a result of the Samurai presence, the practice of kempo moved underground and the art was nurtured in secret. The Japanese brought with them their own samurai battlefield arts (bujitsu). Okinawan martial artists became familiar with these systems, and adopted some of their methods into the evolving Ryukyu version of Chinese kempo.

In addition to the presence of Chinese kempo and Japanese bujitsu, the Okinawan's also possessed an indigenous fighting art known as "te" (or "ti", which means "hand"). This was the art of the Okinawan royal guard, and consisted of pressure point strikes and grappling techniques. Te has continued to be practiced and exists even today.

One of the reasons that te does not enjoy a large following, even in Okinawa, is that its methods became absorbed into the emerging art of Ryukyu kempo. Thus, Chinese kempo formed the basis for a uniquely Okinawan art which incorporated elements of Japanese bujitsu and the methods of te. As a result of this intertwining of cultures, Ryukyu kempo was also called tode-jitsu, a name which acknowledged these sources: "to", referring to the Tang dynasty of China; "de" [te], for the Okinawan element; and "jitsu", the Japanese suffix used to refer to combative disciplines.

(Continued)

Originally, Ryukyu kempo tode-jitsu existed for the sole purpose of self-defense in direct response to various practical necessities. For example, professional security escorts of the day needed to be well-versed in combative technologies. Likewise, the body-guards assigned to the protection of the Okinawan king had to be martial arts experts in order to perform their job. Police officers of ancient Okinawa (no less than their modern counter-parts) also needed realistic and effective fighting methods.

In addition to these professionals for whom martial arts was one of the "tools of the trade," there were also civilian martial artists who studied self-defense against the possibility of a violent encounter (a not-so-unlikely prospect considering the presence of armed samurai). Over the generations, the methods and insights of the professional and civilian martial artists merged as Ryukyu kempo developed.

Because Ryukyu kempo developed for strictly utilitarian reasons, it needed to be a very effective and practical fighting method. At the very heart of Ryukyu kempo's combative approach lie two intertwined arts of exquisite effectiveness — kyusho-jitsu and tuité-jitsu. Kyusho-jitsu is the art of attacking pressure points (the same points used in oriental healing methods). Touches and strikes to these points can result in pain, unconsciousness, and even death. Tuité-jitsu is the art of joint manipulation. Pressure points are used in this art as well, to control and weaken joints, making them vulnerable to attack.

Tuité-jitsu and Kyusho-jitsu are intertwined because the point attacks of kyusho-jitsu create the opportunities for tuité joint maneuvers, and the joint techniques of tuité make openings for decisive blows to exposed pressure points. These methods have been passed on in secret for centuries and may have roots in ancient India, and a secret art called marma adi.

Marma adi is based on methods of attacking 108 vital points. It is known that Chinese martial arts were influenced by Indian martial arts, and so, it is no surprise to find that Chinese kung fu contains two little known, but highly advanced components called dim mak and chin na. Dim mak (or dim hsueh) is the art of attacking vital points and corresponds to kyusho-jitsu. Chin na is the art of manipulating joints and is related to tuité-jitsu.

Together, tuité-jitsu and kyusho-jitsu make Ryukyu kempo a remarkably sophisticated fighting style that depends on knowledge, grace and technique, rather than brute strength. Without proper knowledge and understanding, Ryukyu kempo cannot work (unless the practitioner is extraordinarily strong and athletically gifted, a completely impractical expectation). So, it is amazing that kyusho-jitsu and tuité-jitsu, the two arts which are the very basis of Okinawan combative disciplines, have been virtually unknown to modern karate practitioners. Why is this?

The reason is two-fold. First, though Ryukyu kempo was designed solely for combat, there are other benefits — physical and psychological — of martial arts training. This means that, for those who do not need a fighting art, martial arts can still be enjoyed for these ancillary benefits. And, as we shall see, these benefits can form the rationale for teaching martial arts to the general population.

Second, modern karate is devoid of the combat techniques of kyusho-jitsu and tuité-jitsu because these arts were (as we have mentioned) passed on in secret. Though the practitioners of Ryukyu kempo were sometimes well-known, their methods were carefully guarded. This was to prevent rivals from learning one's methods (or perhaps devising a counter technique), and to keep the most dangerous knowledge out of the hands of untrustworthy individuals. In many cases, a master's most treasured techniques were only divulged to a single student who was the designated successor in the system. Even instructors who were willing to share their knowledge with all their top students usually would wait a long time before even beginning to teach these methods.

There are two oral traditions which illustrate this point. One is that a student would be taught only physical movements for the first ten years, and only after that period of testing and evaluation would he or she be taught the "true art". (This was the case with the late Hohan Soken.) The second tradition is one that simply states that individuals must be at least 35 years old before they are even taught the fundamentals of kyusho-jitsu and tuité-jitsu.

In 1891, so the story goes, two young Ryukyu kempo experts, Chomo Hanashiro (1869-1945) and Kentsu Yabu (1866-1937) — students of Sokon "Bushi" Matsumura (1809-1901), and later of Anko Itosu (1832-1916) — took their army physicals. As this was a time of military expansionism, Japan was vigorously drafting Okinawan men into the army. The military doctors noticed that, unlike other conscripts, Hanashiro and Yabu were exceptionally robust. The two credited their kempo training for their health and vigor. This prompted an investigation into whether Ryukyu kempo might be used to improve the quality of Okinawan draftees.

Around the turn of the century, as a result of this interest by the Japanese military, Anko Itosu (who was also one of Matsumura's students) began a program to teach Ryukyu kempo in the elementary schools.

Itosu detailed his plan for teaching Ryukyu kempo tode-jitsu to children in a letter to the Prefectural Education Department. The letter states, in part, "The purpose of tode is to make the body hard like stones and iron; hands and feet should be used like the points of arrows; hearts should be strong and brave. If children were to practice tode from elementary-school days, they would be well prepared for military service... This will be a great asset to our militaristic society."

Since, kempo was considered far too hazardous for children, he modified the art so that they could not hurt each other. Some of these modifications involved changing the manner in which certain techniques were performed so that they caused no injury — in effect blunting the weapons. Itosu also deleted all teaching of the core methods of Ryukyu kempo, removing both kyusho-jitsu and tuité-jitsu from the curriculum. Instead, he taught the children to block and punch.

Itosu also developed the five simple kata (fixed patterns or forms) called Pinan (Heian in Japanese) and he introduced important philosophical considerations into kempo instruction.

(Continued)

This had the effect of shifting the emphasis in training from combat to personal development. In this way he started a metamorphosis of kempo from bujitsu (martial science) to budo (martial way). To express this change, he proposed a new name for the art, one that was consistent with this new emphasis.

The term to-de (or tou-di) means "Chinese hand" and can also be pronounced kara-te. Itosu proposed replacing the word "to"/"kara" (Chinese) with a different word, also pronounced "kara" but meaning "empty". Thus he argued for the name karate, meaning "emptiness of hand." (This new name, karate-do, was not officially adopted until the mid 30's.) As a result, Itosu became the father of a new martial art — from the combat methods of Ryukyu Kempo tode-jitsu, Itosu created a school-children's budo known as karate-do. (NOTE: Our first book, **KYUSHO-JITSU: The Dillman Method of Pressure Point Fighting,** carefully explains the difference between the "block and punch method" of karate-do and the original Ryukyu kempo fighting methods.)

Itosu recommended teaching his modified art to those training to become school teachers. By teaching the teachers, then sending them out, he hoped to spread his new method. As he explained in his letter, "It is my opinion that all the students of the Okinawa Prefectural Teachers' Training College should practice tode, so that when they graduate from here they can teach children in the schools exactly as I have taught them. Within ten years tode will spread all over Okinawa and to the Japanese mainland."

Itosu's plan succeeded beyond his wildest dreams. Not only did his karate-do spread to the Japanese mainland (it took about 15 years, and was introduced by Itosu's student, Gichin Funakoshi) but eventually it spread to the world. Every practitioner of karate, of kempo and of tae kwon do for that matter, owes Itosu a huge debt of gratitude. Without him, the Okinawan fighting arts would still be a provincial secret.

Because karate-do was an openly practiced art, it quite naturally came to the attention of westerners following WW II. However, when westerners learned the art, they did not appreciate the difference between karate-do and Ryukyu kempo. They believed they were learning a fighting art and not a children's art.

It is easy to understand why this was so; many of the earliest karate instructors were not actually karate practitioners. In fact, they were Ryukyu kempo experts who publicly taught a karate-do curriculum. Often, these instructors would have tremendous reputations as fierce fighters, because they employed Ryukyu kempo's devastating methods. The oriental students of these great masters understood that someday, if they persisted in karate-do training, their sensei (teacher) might take them aside and privately introduce them to the secrets of Ryukyu kempo. Western students, however, did not understand this. They assumed that they were paying for all the secrets these teachers possessed, when in fact, they were merely paying for instruction in karate-do.

This misconception has resulted in frustration and disappointment for countless non-asian martial artists in the last half century. After years of training and dedication, traditional students can find themselves struggling with less-effective (and sometimes completely worthless) fighting skills.

Of course, there is no one to blame for this event. Non-orientals were not (intentionally) misled. After all, Gichin Funakoshi (the founder of Shotokan-ryu, and the "Father of Japanese karate") said it plainly: "The ultimate goal of karate-do lies not in victory or in defeat, but in the perfection of the character of the participant." In contrast, a true combat art is vitally concerned about the issue of victory and defeat, since survival is its reason for being.

This is not to say that karate-do is a bad idea. On the contrary, the school-children's art has proven to be a very beneficial practice for millions. Karate — along with the culturally equivalent arts of tae kwon do and wushu — has grown both in popularity and status as an enjoyable and valuable sport. Karate-do has clearly evolved far beyond its original purpose of preparing school-children for military service.

Unfortunately, most people take up the study of martial arts to learn self-defense. For them, the children's art is not adequate. Also, many martial artists who thrived for years under the aegis of Itosu's revolution reach a point in their personal development when sport and fitness are no longer the prime concerns of training — a point when the issues of self-defense and real combat move to the forefront. What is there for them? How can they regain the original intent of the Okinawan fighting traditions?

The answer is to reintroduce kyusho-jitsu and tuité-jitsu into karate training. And the avenue for this reintroduction is through kata. Kata are the formal exercises of karate. They consist of fixed patterns of movements. In karate-do, kata is described as a series of blocks, punches, and kicks. Ryukyu kempo sees kata as an almost inexhaustible collection of pressure point and grappling techniques.

The body is covered with kyusho, vital points, or pressure points — also called tsubo, a shiatsu term. These points are used in acupuncture, moxibustion, and massage to promote health and healing. These same points can be used to hurt. Because the points are highly responsive, strength is not required to effectively utilize them. This makes pressure point fighting a highly efficient form of combat.

In acupuncture, the needle must be inserted correctly, and manipulated properly for any given point to work. Likewise, in kyusho-jitsu and tuité-jitsu the proper angle and method of activation for each pressure point must be employed to obtain the desired effect. For this reason, instruction on pressure point fighting must include not only the location of the points, but also information on the proper use of each point.

The movements of traditional kata contain this required information. Each move is a self-defense technique that precisely maps out the proper points to use and the correct method of using them. This is why kata training has always stressed technical precision as one of its values. In karate-do it has simply been assumed that this interest in precision was merely part of the discipline of the art, a never-ending quest for perfection. In fact, the precision is important to insure that pressure points are properly attacked in real combat.

Kata only works if there is a deep understanding of its meaning. And this is the key to

(Continued)

restoring the original combative quality of Ryukyu kempo to the grade-school art of karate-do. To do this, one needs to study kyusho-jitsu and tuité-jitsu and come to an understanding of their basic principles. Then, one should analyze the traditional forms to determine the pressure point techniques which they contain. This is called "bunkai," or application.

Finally, by visualizing these applications when doing the form, and by taking the time to practice the applications with a partner, the old methods can come to life again.

This is our purpose in presenting these texts. In **KYUSHO-JITSU: The Dillman Method of Pressure Point Fighting,** we explain the difference between karate-do and tode-jitsu, and reveal the fundamentals of kyusho-jitsu. In **Advanced Pressure Point Fighting of RYUKYU KEMPO,** we explain the underlying principles and advanced techniques of kyusho-jitsu. In this text, we present the secrets of tuité-jitsu.

With the knowledge and concepts presented, mature martial artists — even though trained in the school-children's karate-do — can examine their own arts and rediscover the older combative approach of Ryukyu kempo tode-jitsu. In this way karate-ka who have outgrown the children's training can practice a more mature and effective art.

BIBLIOGRAPHY & HISTORICAL SOURCES FOR CHAPTER ONE

BISHOP, Mark.
  Okinawan Karate, Teachers, Styles and Secret Techniques,
  A & C Black, Ltd., London, 1989

FUNAKOSHI, Gichin
  Karate-do Kyohan, Kodansha International, Tokyo, Japan, 1973
  Karate-do Nyumon, Kodansha International, Tokyo, Japan, 1988

McCARTHY, Patrick.
  The Bubishi: a Translation and Analysis, 3rd ed.,
  International Ryukyu Karate Research Society, Yokohama, Japan, 1994

NAGAMINE, Shoshin.
  The Essence of Okinawan Karate-do, Charles E. Tuttle, Rutland, Vermont, 1976

NOTE ON THE TERM "DILLMAN METHOD"

In the martial arts it is common for senior martial artists to open their own dojo. If they are successful at this, they will sometimes end up as the head of a martial arts organization. When such a person has learned from more than one master, it is not at all uncommon to find him teaching a version of the art which is not exactly what any one of his teachers taught, but which does contain elements of all. When this occurs a delicate issue arises concerning the proper name for the art which is being taught.

As a matter of respect, a teacher will sometimes use the name of the art which one of his masters taught him. However, it would be disrespectful to use the name without in some way distinguishing it from his master's art. One way in which this is done is to use the term "ha" or family. For example, Hayashi-ha Shito-ryu refers to that version of the style Shito-ryu taught by T. Hayashi.

The term Ryukyu Kempo was not known in the United States (except among a few martial arts historians) until Seiyu Oyata began teaching and using that name for his art. Master Oyata was a very important teacher of George Dillman. In fact, it was Mr. Oyata who wrote the original calligraphy which appears on our uniform-patches. Though Dillman has had many teachers whose influences appear in what he teaches, he has continued to use the name Ryukyu kempo as a sign of respect. However, rather than using the awkward sounding Japanese phrasing, Dillman-ha Ryukyu kempo, we have chosen the more familiar English term "Dillman Method."

WARNING

This is an educational book, but these techniques are NOT TO BE PERFORMED WITHOUT PROPER SUPERVISION. We want to share our years of experience with you, but we do not want anyone injured. It is essential that you consult a physician regarding whether or not to attempt any technique in this book. Always have a Dillman Method Instructor supervise your practice.

Mike Solecki at 6'5" uses a finger lock on larger opponent Todd Quann.

PRINCIPLES OF TUITÉ

The old art of Ryukyu kempo can be divided into two interrelated aspects. These are kyusho-jitsu (kyoo-sho-jit-soo) and tuité-jitsu (too-ee-tay-jit-soo). Kyusho-jitsu is the art of attacking pressure points. In fact, this is what the name means — kyusho means "vital point" or "pressure point", and jitsu means "fighting art".

Tuité-jitsu (tuité means "grasping hand" and is also pronounced torite) is an art devoted to controlling or injuring an opponent by the manipulation of the joints. The key to tuité-jitsu is the manipulation which takes place before the joint is locked out. Tuité-waza (waza means "combat technique") apply a variety of strategies to neutralize the body's ability to protect the joints from injury. Once this is accomplished, the joint is completely vulnerable and can be locked or dislocated with minimal effort.

Kyusho-jitsu and tuité-jitsu are inter-related in two ways. First, kyusho-jitsu and tuité-jitsu are part of a single combative response continuum. In other words, a Ryukyu kempo self-defense method will involve both kyusho-waza (pressure-point attack) and tuité-waza (joint attack) in rapid succession. A rule of thumb is, **strike a point to attack a joint; attack a joint to strike a point.**

Second, the most important means of neutralizing the natural defenses of a joint is to stimulate the pressure points which control the joint (see below). So, attacking vital points — which is the definition of kyusho-jitsu — is central in tuité-jitsu.

When studying an art like tuité-jitsu it is important to go beyond the techniques, and seek to understand the principles behind them. The reason for this is that it is not possible to develop oneself as a martial artist without understanding the concepts which govern one's art. A person who only knows how to do a technique, but not why it works, cannot develop further techniques, or respond creatively to circumstances which do not fit the exact scenario used in practice.

Therefore, it is not our desire that readers should simply parrot our methods. Rather, our wish is that readers should become creative contributors to the total body of martial arts knowledge. For this reason, we will explain principles of tuité before anything else. And, we encourage readers to reread the principles after studying the techniques in this book, because it is in the application of the techniques that the concepts become alive and relevant.

9 PRINCIPLES OF TUITE´

The entire secret of tuité-jitsu can be summed up in one sentence: **create vulnerability in a joint, then seize that advantage and attack the joint.** The principles of tuité are methods of creating that vulnerability and insuring the outcome of the technique. It is these principles which make tuité-waza virtually 100% effective.

1. Use Pressure Points

Every joint of the body is controlled by at least four pressure points [PHOTOS A & B]. By properly stimulating any one of them, a joint can be made to involuntarily bend, or straighten. This result can be explained in terms of reflexes.

Reflexes are safety responses designed to move an endangered body part away from a threat. It takes too long for the brain to look, think and then react to a threatening stimuli. As a result, the reflexes bypass the brain altogether. Stimulating a vital point sends a message into the body that is interpreted by the reflexes as a threat. The reflexes respond by trying to move the joint out of danger. To accomplish this, the "threatened" joint and the next joint nearer the body (proximal) relax and move away from the stimulus [PHOTOS C-E].

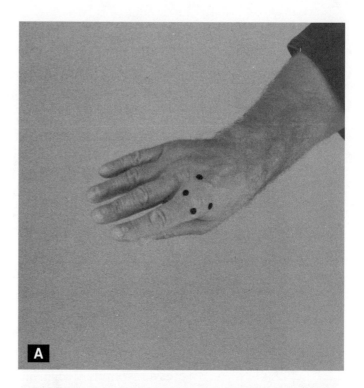

A

D

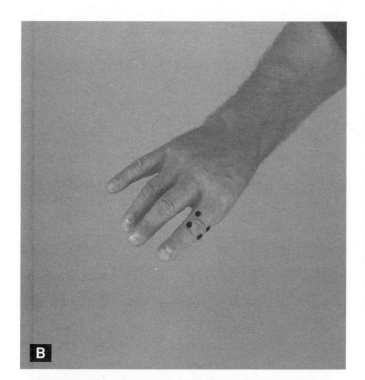

(Continued)

However, once the joints have relaxed, they no longer have any muscular resistance against the application of a joint technique. Also, once a joint is in motion, it is easily controlled by keeping it in motion. In other words, **the safety response of the body creates the very circumstances which make the joints helpless against attack.** This means that tuité techniques can be applied successfully on opponents of any size.

Another way in which pressure points work is by disrupting the flow of vital energy (ki). For example, neither the pressure point Lung # 5 (at the crease of the elbow) nor Pericardium # 2, (on the biceps) directly controls the wrist. Yet, a strike to either of these points can stop the flow of energy to the entire arm, thereby weakening the wrist and making it vulnerable to attack.

Similarly, a strike to Triple Warmer # 17 (located behind the jaw) can disrupt the flow of energy to the brain, resulting in disorientation or even unconsciousness. Obviously, a dazed opponent is helpless against the application of a joint attack. This highlights an essential relationship between tuité-jitsu and kyusho-jitsu, which will be evident in many of the self-defense techniques presented in the later chapters.

2. Utilize Two-way Action

Two-way action means to pull and push at the same time. Pull the base of the finger forward and push the tip of the finger back to lock the finger. Press at the elbow and pull at the wrist to lock the elbow [PHOTO A-C]. It is possible for the brain to resist one movement, but very difficult for the brain to resist two.

NOTE: This idea is very important in Wally Jay's Small Circle Jujitsu.

(Continued)

3. Apply Complex Torque

Complex torque means to move a joint in more than one direction, and can be described as "bend and twist". In the case of a finger lock, the finger is bent, then turned [PHOTOS D-F]. The body can defend against bending or twisting, but not against both at the same time.

NOTE: This principle will work even on double-jointed individuals.

(Continued)

4. Generate Confusion

Create vulnerability in the opponent by confusing the mind or by confusing the joint itself. The mind can be confused by almost any means that will take the opponent's attention away from the joint you intend to manipulate. Just before doing a tuité-waza, a slap, a strike, even a sudden shout (kiai) can be enough to make the joint technique easy to apply. For example, when grabbed by the arms, kick the attacker's leg, then apply a wrist turn/press [PHOTO A-D].

The joint itself can be confused by moving it in several different directions before applying the lock. Sometimes moving in just one separate direction is all that is necessary. Wiggling a joint, or manipulating it in a circle are also very effective.

Another method of confusion is a tuité progression. In a tuité progression the joint is manipulated into one tuité technique, but not maintained there. Immediately, one technique gives way to another. When the first technique is applied, the opponent's whole body begins to move. When the next technique is applied in rapid succession, the body must react by moving in a completely different direction. By applying one technique, then immediately switching to another, the opponent's body is so confused that he becomes helpless. (see chapter four)

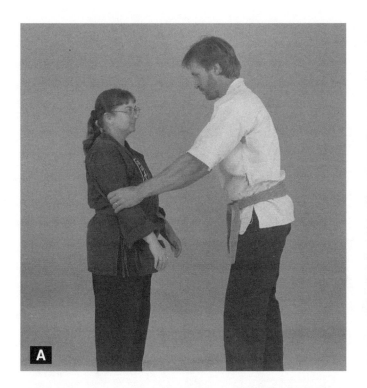

(Continued)

5. Work Against a Base

When a joint technique begins to be effective, the opponent's body naturally moves away from the pressure. By working against a base, you create resistance in opposition to the opponent's natural escaping action. The joint becomes trapped between your hand applying the technique and this base. Generally a base is created by locking against your second hand, or your leg [PHOTOS A-B].

6. Create Mechanical Advantage

To be as effective as possible you must maximize your mechanical advantage. This principle means to position yourself where you are strongest and where the opponent is weakest. Keeping your arms close to your own body is mechanically the strongest position for you. When your arms are extended you are weak. This means that when applying a technique, you should generally step into the attack, or pull the opponent in toward you, in order to use your natural strength.

Also, when attacking an opponent, there are certain angles that are mechanically weaker on him. When executing a movement, you may need to move to your opponent's side, or position yourself on a diagonal. For example, when applying the basic wrist turn/press (see chapter four for technical details) it is easy for the opponent to resist when you stand directly in front of him [PHOTO A]. However, once you move diagonally to his outside he becomes helpless against you [PHOTO B-C]. These angles vary depending on the technique being employed, so they are learned in conjunction with individual moves.

(Continued)

33

7. Apply Variable Pressure

Another principle of tuité´ is the use of variable pressure. When applying a joint technique, exert pressure to lock the joint. Then, as the opponent tries to resist, suddenly release the pressure. The opponent's body will begin to relax. As he relaxes, apply the pressure again. By working the joint in an on/off manner, the joint can be rendered helpless.

This principle is especially useful in restraint techniques. If you use tuité´ to hold or pin an assailant and maintain constant, even pressure, initially he will experience pain. But, in less than a minute, his body will grow accustomed to the pain, and he will be able to get out of the hold! [PHOTOS A-B] If, however, you vary the amount of pressure on the joint, always keeping enough pressure to maintain control, while at the same time increasing and decreasing the level of pain, his body will not be able to adapt. In fact your opponent will experience intense pain and will be completely helpless [PHOTOS C-D].

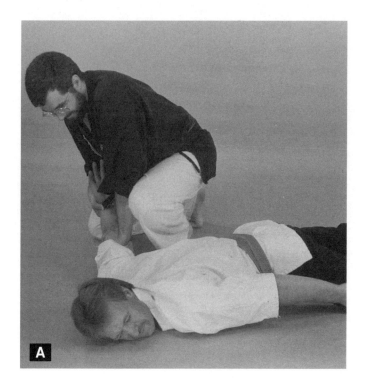

A

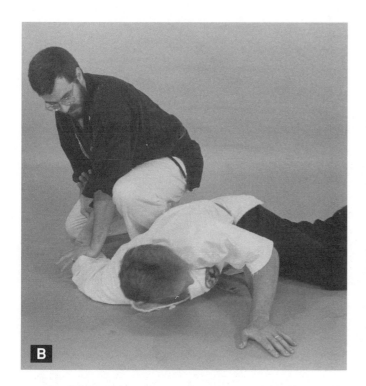

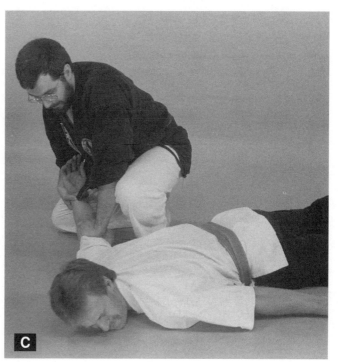

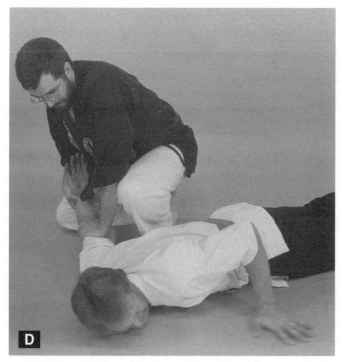

(Continued)

8. Stick to the Opponent

An essential concept in all aspects of traditional karate is to stick or adhere to an opponent, without actually grabbing. This is called muchimi in Okinawan. Muchimi is mostly done with the forearms, though other parts of the body (in particular, the legs) are also used. In tuité, you stick to your opponent in order to control and direct his body into the joint attack. For example, if an opponent reaches with two hands, you can control him by sticking to his wrist and circling his hand into position for a finger lock [PHOTOS A-E]. It is even possible to lock an opponent without grabbing, just by controlling and pressing with the arms and body [PHOTO F].

9. Utilize Redundancy

Redundancy means to apply several principles at the same time or in rapid succession. In fact, several of the principles already mentioned have redundant factors. For example, a strike to a pressure point on the biceps will stop the flow of energy, but the pain of the blow also serves as a distraction, which creates confusion in the opponent's mind. This one strike fulfills the purpose of two different principles. Conversely, even if the strike misses the pressure point, it still serves to distract and confuse.

What happens if a joint attack is made using pressure point strikes to disrupt ki flow, and pressure point manipulation to release the joint, and two-way action with complex torque to overcome the joint's protective resistance, and variable pressure to insure that the opponent cannot adapt to the level of pain? The answer is that it becomes a virtually 100% technique. Even if the defender fails to accurately perform one or more aspects of the movement due to the stress of a violent encounter, those movements which are successfully executed will suffice. This is the principle of redundancy: a technique will work even when it is not done perfectly.

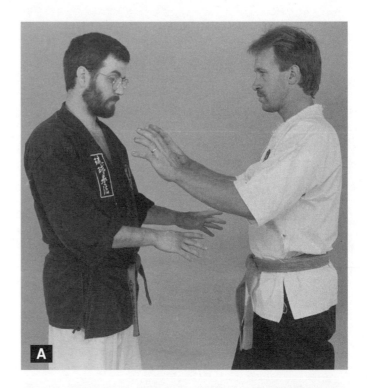

A

D

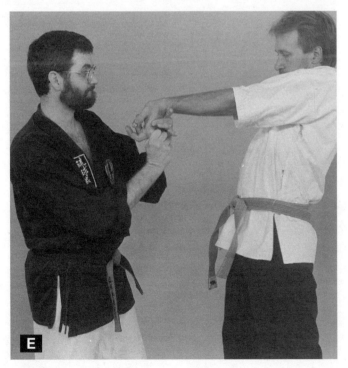

Ron Richards uses pressure points and grappling to drop Kevin Rice during a seminar in Emmaus, PA.

THE PRESSURE POINTS

THE INTERRELATIONSHIP BETWEEN TUITÉ-JITSU & KYUSHO-JITSU

A look at most modern karate instruction suggests that karate is a method of striking and kicking. A look at judo or aikido suggests that these arts are grappling methods. The impression one gets is that methods of striking and methods of grappling are essentially incompatible. Nothing could be further from the truth. Striking and joint-manipulation are different aspects of the same art of Ryukyu kempo.

In kyusho-jitsu, pressure points are targeted and struck to produce pain, altered awareness or unconsciousness. In tuité-jitsu pressure points are touched to release joints for painful manipulation or breaking. Pressure points are interrelated, and work together. One point "sets-up" another, making it more vulnerable and sensitive to attack.

This means that a strike aimed at a certain pressure point will activate a second point used in a joint technique. Conversely, a well executed joint technique will sensitize a point on the body which is to be struck. The techniques of kyusho-jitsu and tuité-jitsu flow freely from one to the other and back again.

Therefore a key task in learning Ryukyu kempo is to learn the location and proper method for activation of the many pressure points of the body. There are 361 pressure points used in traditional acupuncture, and shiatsu (plus roughly 350 more "extraordinary" points identified by modern acupuncturists). These are the points used in kyusho-jitsu and tuité-jitsu. However, though all 361 plus points could be used for combat, only the most practical are. This amounts to roughly 120 of the total number of points (some sources say 108, of which 36 are lethal).

The pressure points lie on pathways called meridians. These pathways mark the course that vital-energy, or ki, travels through the body. The various meridians are related to various bodily organs. These are - lung, large intestine, stomach, spleen, heart, small intestine, bladder, kidney, pericardium, triple warmer (an "organ" in Chinese medicine, sometimes identified with the thyroid), gall bladder, and liver. In addition to these twelve channels (which are bilateral, that is, on both the right and left sides of the body), there are also two centerline meridians. These are called the conception and governor meridians.

The energy in the body has a flow, outward and inward, up and down. And this flow expresses a kind of polarity, similar to the properties of positive and negative electrical potential. In Chinese this polarity is called yin and yang.

MERIDIAN	ELEMENT	POLARITY
Lung	Metal	Yin
Large Intestine	Metal	Yang
Stomach	Earth	Yang
Spleen	Earth	Yin
Heart	Fire	Yin
Small Intestine	Fire	Yang
Bladder	Water	Yang
Kidney	Water	Yin
Pericardium	Fire	Yin
Triple Warmer	Fire	Yang
Gall Bladder	Wood	Yang
Liver	Wood	Yin

As the yin and yang energy travels through each meridian, it expresses a characteristic of that channel called its elemental value. There are five of these elemental values — namely: earth, water, fire, metal and wood.

These elements are intended to describe the ways in which the various meridians interact. Each element has a destructive effect on one other element in the cycle. For example, fire destroys metal, and fire is destroyed by water. In the same manner, each element has a constructive effect on one other. Fire creates earth, and fire is created by wood.

The techniques of pressure point fighting capitalize on these characteristics. Because each meridian is either yin or yang, attacks are aimed in such a manner that a yin meridian is "shorted out" by a mated yang meridian. Because each meridian has an elemental value (except the two centerline channels), they are attacked in the order of the cycle of destruction. And, because energy flows through the meridians in the first place, attacks are aimed in such a manner that ki flow is disrupted. This is the essence of pressure point fighting, to disrupt the flow of ki.

In **KYUSHO-JITSU: The Dillman Method of Pressure Point Fighting,** we explain the fundamentals of pressure points, and in **Advanced Pressure Point Fighting of RYUKYU KEMPO,** we provide careful detail about these principles and concepts. While we feel it is important for readers to be familiar with the material in those texts, we have written this book so that it is able to stand alone. Therefore, this chapter covers every pressure point which is used in this text. Further, in our self-defense examples, we have also pointed out the principles being applied to disrupt ki flow. Readers who desire more information on points and their applications should refer to our other texts.

George A. Dillman, knocks out Ron Houck during an Ohio seminar at Heidelberg College, Tiffin, Ohio. (photo by Michael Ruppert)

NOTE TO READER

Careless or excessive pressure point practice can be dangerous, therefore, the following rules of training must be strictly observed.

1. **Train only under a qualified instructor.**
2. **Do not work on pressure points for more than fifteen minutes per week.**
3. **When training, do not switch sides. Only strike on one side of the body in any given training session.**
4. **Do not apply cross-body techniques, that is: do not strike corresponding points on opposite sides of your partner's body.**
5. **Be sure to learn proper revival techniques.**
6. **Do not work pressure points on persons with health problems, or people over the age of 40, or people on drugs (legal or otherwise).**
7. **Use the utmost restraint at all times. <u>It is not necessary to knock someone out cold to see the effect of a pressure point.</u> Usually a light blow is sufficient to demonstrate effectiveness.**

A standard acupuncture numbering system is being used to designate various pressure points. This is to assist the reader to research further by referring to texts on acupuncture. In describing these points, the designation AU will often appear. AU stands for Anatomical Unit. This is a "body inch" or cun in Chinese. The AU is different for every person, but the average length 1 AU = 1/2 - 1 inch. One AU is equal to the width of the thumb at the joint.

PRESSURE POINT LOCATIONS AND USES

HEART # 8: H-8   [FIG. 1]
LOCATION: On the palm of the hand between the 4th and 5th metacarpals, in the fourth lumbrical muscle and the tendon of the digitorum sublimis muscle. When the hand is closed into a (loose) fist, the tip of the little finger rests on this point.
ANATOMY: The common palmar digital artery and vein, and the fourth common palmar digital branch of the ulnar nerve.
METHOD: Press with the fingertips. [A-B]

Lung # 10: L-10   [FIG. 1]
LOCATION: Located at about the mid-point of the first metacarpal, on the thenar prominence in the lateral abductor pollicis brevis and opponens pollicis muscles. It is found in the "meat of the thumb" on the borderline between the (reddish) skin of the palm and the skin of the back of the hand.
ANATOMY: A branch of the cephalic vein of the thumb, the lateral cutaneous nerve of the forearm and a superficial branch of the radial nerve.
METHOD: Press with the fingertips. [C-D]

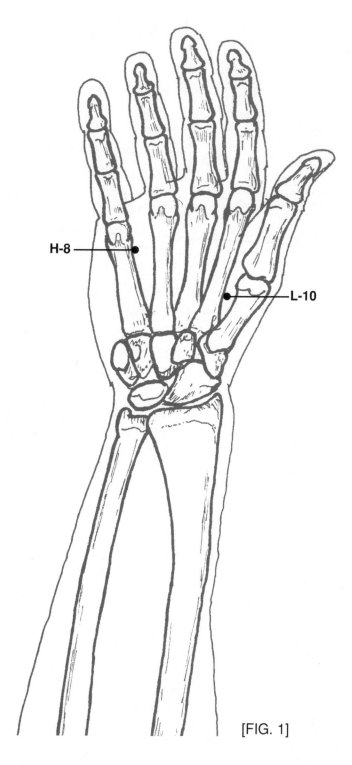

[FIG. 1]

(Continued)

LUNG # 7: L-7 [FIG. 2]
LOCATION: 1.5 AU from the crease of the wrist, in the depression just behind the bony prominence (styloid process) of the radius, on the thumb side of the forearm.
ANATOMY: The lateral antebrachial cutaneous nerve, the superficial ramus of the radial nerve, and the cephalic vein.
METHOD: This point may be pressed, or struck toward the wrist to weaken the hand.

LUNG # 8: L-8   [FIG. 2]
LOCATION: One AU proximal to the crease of the wrist in the depression by the radial artery (the place a nurse takes a pulse).
ANATOMY: The lateral antebrachial cutaneous nerve, the superficial ramus of the radial nerve.
METHOD: Press into the depression next to the radial bone, and up toward the wrist to weaken the hand.

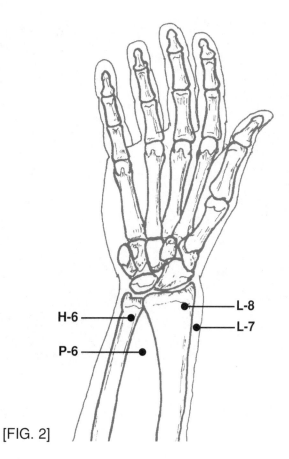

[FIG. 2]

HEART # 6: H-6 [FIG. 2]
LOCATION: 1/2 AU proximal from the crease of the wrist, on the inside (palmar aspect) of the forearm, against the ulnar bone and next to the tendon of the flexor carpi ulnaris.
ANATOMY: The ulnar nerve, and the medial antebrachial cutaneous nerve.
METHOD: Push this point against the ulnar bone and toward the hand to weaken the grip and the wrist.

PERICARDIUM # 6: P-6 [FIG. 2]
LOCATION: Between the tendons of the flexor carpi radialis and the flexor digitorum sublimis muscle two AU proximal to the center of the transverse crease in the wrist. This point can be found in the soft space between the tendons of the wrist.
ANATOMY: The medial and lateral cutaneous nerves of the forearm. This point lies directly on the medial nerve.
METHOD: Press in and toward the fist to weaken the hand.

M-UE-22: 3 Extraordinary points [FIG. 3]

LOCATION: In the web of the fingers, between the metacarpalphalangeal joints of the index, middle, ring and little fingers of the hand.
ANATOMY: Above the dorsal digital and common palmar digital nerves.
METHOD: Use these points to release the fingers, by pressing and stretching them toward the digit to be manipulated.

LARGE INTESTINE # 2: LI-2 [FIG. 3]
LOCATION: In the depression of the bone, 1/2 AU distal to the metacarpalphalangeal joint, on the lateral margin of the dorsal surface of the second digit. This point is located in the depression on the outside of the bone of the index finger just beyond knuckle.
ANATOMY: The dorsal digital branch of the radial nerve, and the palmar digital proprial branch of the medial nerve.
METHOD: Press this point diagonally toward the knuckle to release the finger.

LARGE INTESTINE # 3: LI-3 [FIG. 3]
LOCATION: In the depression of the bone, 1/2 AU proximal to the metacarpalphalangeal joint, on the lateral margin of the dorsal surface of the second metacarpal. This point is located in the depression on the back of the hand, just behind and to the outside of the knuckle of the index finger.
ANATOMY: The superficial ramus of the radial nerve.
METHOD: Press this point diagonally toward the knuckle to release the finger.

M-UE-50: Extraordinary Point [FIG. 3]
LOCATION: In the depression between the third and fourth metacarpal, proximal to the third and fourth metacarpalphalangeal joints. It is found on the back of the hand, just behind and between the knuckles of the middle and ring fingers.
ANATOMY: Above the dorsal digital and common palmar digital nerves.
METHOD: Press this point diagonally toward the knuckle of the third or fourth finger to release it.

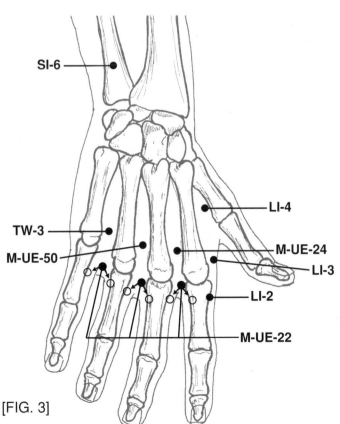

[FIG. 3]

TRIPLE WARMER # 3: TW-3 [FIG. 3]
LOCATION: 1 AU proximal to the metacarpalphalangeal joints (knuckles) between the 4th and 5th metacarpals on the dorsal aspect of the hand in the fourth interosseous muscle. It is on the back of the hand, about one third of the distance from the knuckles to the wrist, between the bones of the fourth and fifth fingers.
ANATOMY: A dorsal branch of the ulnar nerve.
METHOD: Press this point with the thumb. It may also be struck to immobilize the hand.

M-UE-24: Extraordinary Point [FIG. 3]
LOCATION: 1/2 AU proximal to the metacarpalphalangeal joints (knuckles) between the 2nd and 3rd metacarpals on the dorsal aspect of the hand in the interosseous muscle of the second metacarpus. It is on the back of the hand, between the bones of the index and middle fingers, in the hollow behind the knuckles.
ANATOMY: The deep terminal branch of the ulnar nerve.
METHOD: Press this point with the thumb when performing a wrist reversal technique. Press diagonally toward the index or middle knuckle to release that finger.

LARGE INTESTINE # 4: LI-4 [FIG. 3]
LOCATION: In the dorsal interosseous muscle between the 1st and 2nd metacarpals. It is in the "web of the thumb" slightly toward the bone of the index finger.
ANATOMY: A superficial branch of the radial nerve.
METHOD: Press this point firmly against the side of the index finger bone (2nd metacarpal).

SMALL INTESTINE # 6: SI-6 [FIG. 3]
LOCATION: 1/2 AU proximal to the crease of the wrist on the back (dorsal aspect) of the forearm, in the cleft of the bony nob (styloid process) of the ulna.
ANATOMY: The dorsal branch of the ulnar nerve, and branches of the posterior antebrachial cutaneous nerve.
METHOD: Press this point against the bone and toward the hand to bend the wrist.

LUNG # 6: L-6 [FIG 4]

LOCATION: On the radial aspect of the forearm, 6 AU proximal to the crease of the wrist, in the brachioradialis muscle. This point can be found on the thumb-side of the arm about halfway between the wrist and the elbow.

ANATOMY: The lateral cutaneous nerve of the forearm and a superficial branch of the radial nerve.

METHOD: Strike this point toward the fist to weaken the fist.

LUNG # 5: L-5 [FIG 4]

LOCATION: At the crease of the elbow, just lateral to the biceps tendon at the origin of the brachioradialis muscle.

ANATOMY: Branches of the radial recurrent artery and vein and the lateral cutaneous nerve of the forearm, directly above the main trunk of the radial nerve.

METHOD: Strike in a circular manner that cuts back toward the hand. This point may also be pressed with the tip of the thumb.

HEART # 2: H-2 [FIG 4]

LOCATION: Three AU proximal to the inside end of the crease of the elbow, in the space between the biceps and the triceps.

ANATOMY: The superior ulnar collateral artery, the medial antebrachial cutaneous nerve and the ulnar nerve.

METHOD: Strike or grab to bend the elbow.

PERICARDIUM # 2: P-2 [FIG 4]

LOCATION: Two AU distal to the level of the fold of the armpit (axillary crease) along the mid-line of the biceps.

ANATOMY: The muscular branches of the brachial artery, the medial brachial cutaneous nerve and the musculocutaneous nerve.

METHOD: Strike toward the bone (humerus) to numb the biceps.

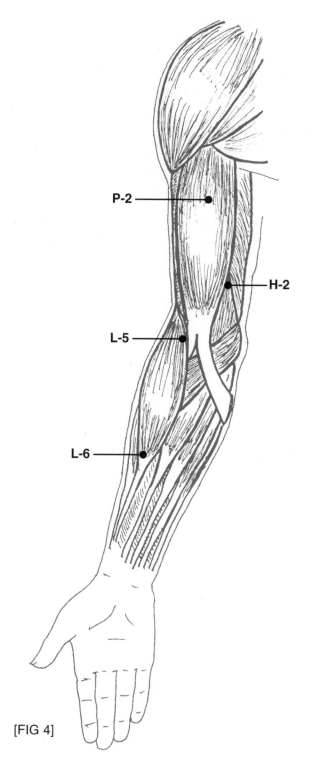

[FIG 4]

SMALL INTESTINE # 7: SI-7 [FIG. 5]
LOCATION: In the middle of the forearm, 5 AU proximal to the wrist along the ulna at the end of the extensor carpi ulnaris muscle.
ANATOMY: The branch of the medial antebrachial cutaneous nerve; more deeply, the posterior interosseous nerve.
METHOD: Strike or press this point against the ulnar bone. A strike will open the hand.

LARGE INTESTINE # 7: LI-7 [FIG. 5]
LOCATION: About 5 AU proximal to the wrist on the thumb side of the forearm.
ANATOMY: The posterior antebrachial cutaneous nerve and the deep ramus of the radial nerve.
METHOD: Strike this point against the bone, in the direction of the hand.

TRIPLE WARMER # 11: TW-11   [FIG. 5]
LOCATION: Two AU above the tip of the elbow on the tendon of the triceps.
ANATOMY: The posterior brachial nerve, the muscular branch of the radial nerve, and the Body of Golgi's nerve receptor.
METHOD: Rub this point using an up and down motion to hyper-extend the elbow and lock the shoulder.

TRIPLE WARMER # 12: TW-12   [FIG. 5]
LOCATION: In the middle of the triceps.
ANATOMY: The median collateral artery, the posterior brachial cutaneous nerve, and the muscular branch of the radial nerve. This point also lies over the fuciform fiber of the humerus bone.
METHOD: Strike this point against the bone to release the shoulder and lock the elbow.

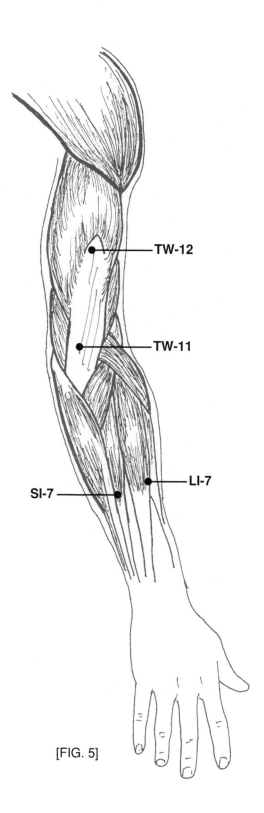

[FIG. 5]

(Continued)

LARGE INTESTINE # 10: LI-10 [FIG. 6]

LOCATION: 2 AU distal from the <u>outside end</u> of the crease of the elbow (the lateral end of the transverse cubital crease), between the supinator longus muscle (also called the brachioradialus) and the extensor carpi radialis longus. It is approximately one AU distal from the elbow joint on the outside of the forearm.

ANATOMY: The muscular branch of the musculo-spiral nerve, the antebrachial cutaneous nerve; a deep branch of the radial nerve.

METHOD: Strike this point to produce numbness in the arm.

LARGE INTESTINE # 11: LI-11 [FIG. 6]

LOCATION: On the radial aspect of the elbow, at the origin of the extensor carpi radialis muscle and the radial side of the brachioradialis muscle. This point can be found just to the outside of the crease of the elbow at the bulge of the muscle.

ANATOMY: The posterior cutaneous nerve and the radial nerve trunk.

METHOD: Strike this point back to front to produce numbness in the arm.

> **NOTE: Because of the close proximity and similar function of LI-10 and LI-11, these points are essentially interchangeable in combat.**

LARGE INTESTINE # 13: LI-13 [FIG. 6]

LOCATION: In the hollow depression near the distal end of the biceps, about three AU proximal to the lateral epicondyle of the humerus (the outer knob of the elbow).

ANATOMY: The radial collateral artery, the posterior antebrachial cutaneous nerve and the radial nerve.

METHOD: Hit this point against the underlying bone (humerus) to bend the arm inward and cause numbing and pain down the arm to the end of the thumb. This point also responds to pressing.

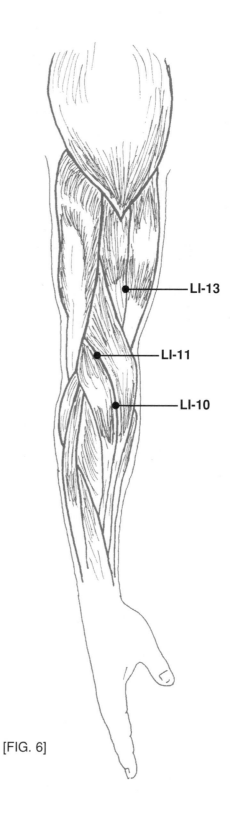

LI-13

LI-11

LI-10

[FIG. 6]

CONCEPTION # 22: Co-22 [FIG. 7]
LOCATION: In the hollow depression above the suprasternal notch.
ANATOMY: Anterior branch of the supraclavicular nerve.
METHOD: With one or two fingers, press in and down. [PHOTOS A-B]

> **CAUTION: Pressing straight in or with an upward motion can damage the trachea.**

STOMACH # 9: S-9 [FIG. 7]
LOCATION: At the meeting of the anterior border of the sternocleidomastoid and the thyroid cartilage, level with the laryngeal prominence. It is level with the Adam's apple, at the crease of the neck muscle.
ANATOMY: The bifurcation of the carotid arteries, the cutaneous colli nerve, a cervical branch of the facial (seventh cranial) nerve, and the vagus nerve.
METHOD: Strike with a penetrating blow on a 45 degree angle into the neck to produce unconsciousness.

STOMACH # 10: S-10 [FIG. 7]
LOCATION: At the anterior margin of the sternocleidomastoid, midway between S-9 and the clavicle.
ANATOMY: Cutaneous cervical nerve, the superior cardiac nerve.
METHOD: Strike in combination with S-9 to produce unconsciousness.

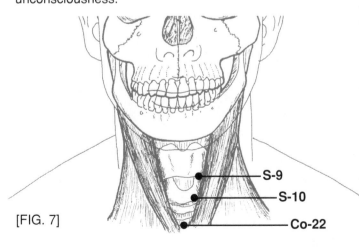

[FIG. 7]
S-9
S-10
Co-22

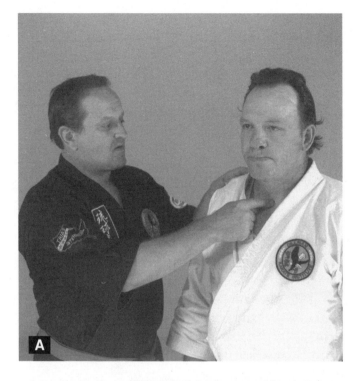

A

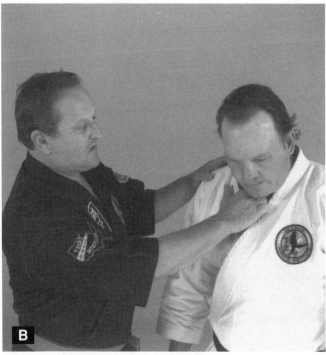

B

(Continued)

LARGE INTESTINE # 18: LI-18 [FIG. 8]

LOCATION: 3 AU lateral to the laryngeal prominence, in the posterior margin of the sternocleidomastoid. It can be found on the side of the neck, level with the Adam's apple and directly below the ear.

ANATOMY: The ascending cervical artery, the great auricular nerve, the cutaneous colli nerve, the lesser occipital nerve and the accessory nerve.

METHOD: Strike this point when the neck is bent toward one side, and the sternocleidomastoid muscle is stretched.

SMALL INTESTINE # 16: SI-16 [FIG. 8]

LOCATION: On the posterior border of the sternocleidomastoid, 1 AU posterior to LI-18. This point lies on the side of the neck, level with the Adam's apple, and just behind the muscle.

ANATOMY: The ascending cervical artery, the cutaneous cervical nerve, and the emerging portion of the great auricular nerve.

METHOD: With the opponent's head turned slightly, strike this point at about a 30 degree angle from back to front.

TRIPLE WARMER # 17: TW-17 [FIG. 8]

LOCATION: Behind the jaw, in the depression under the ear.

ANATOMY: The posterior auricular artery, the superficial jugular vein, the great auricular nerve and the facial (seventh cranial) nerve at its point of emergence from the stylomastoid foramen.

METHOD: Strike diagonally back to front, hitting the point against the back of the jaw-bone, resulting in unconsciousness.

> **CAUTION: A blow at TW-17 can dislocate the jaw.**

SMALL INTESTINE # 17: SI-17 [FIG. 8]

LOCATION: Posterior to the angle of the mandible in the anterior margin at the insertion of the sternocleidomastoid muscle. It is located in the depression behind the corner of the jaw.

ANATOMY: The internal carotid artery, a branch of the great auricular nerve, a cervical branch of the facial (seventh cranial) nerve, and a superior cervical ganglion of the sympathetic trunk.

METHOD: Strike on an upward 45 degree angle toward the center of the head.

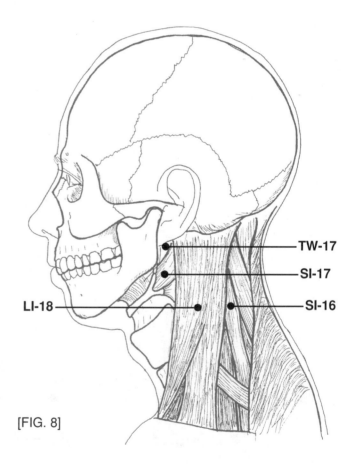

[FIG. 8]

STOMACH # 5: S-5 [FIG. 9]

LOCATION: Anterior to the angle of the mandible, on the anterior border of the masseter muscle, at the groove of the jaw. It is found at the notch along the bottom of the jaw.

ANATOMY: The facial artery and the buccal nerve.

METHOD: Hit this point on a line 45 degrees toward the center of the head.

STOMACH # 7: S-7   [FIG. 9]

LOCATION: In the hollow of the temporomandibular joint, at the origin of the masseter muscle. It is in the depression at the hinge of the jaw.

ANATOMY: Zygomaticoorbital branch of the facial nerve, and a branch of the auriculotemporal nerve.

METHOD: Hit this point 45 degrees downward to dislocate the jaw.

CAUTION: Never actually hit S-7 in practice.

SMALL INTESTINE # 18: SI-18 [FIG. 9]

LOCATION: At the mid-point of the inferior margin of the zygomatic bone, directly below the outer canthus of the eye. It lies in the depression below the prominence of the cheekbone, in front of the masseter (the muscle which bulges when clenching the jaw).

ANATOMY: The transverse facial artery, the facial (seventh cranial) nerve and the infraorbital nerve.

METHOD: Strike or press on an upward diagonal line toward the center of the head causing the neck to release.

Triple Warmer # 23: TW-23   [FIG. 9]

LOCATION: In the oricularis oculi muscle, on the lateral border of the zygomatic process of the frontal bone. It is at the end of the eyebrow in the depression of the temple.

ANATOMY: The zygomaticotemporalis nerve.

METHOD: Strike with a small surface, such as a middle-knuckle fist, from the side, and slightly forward.

CAUTION: Never actually hit TW-23 in practice.

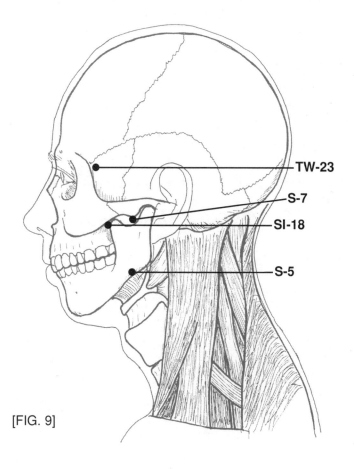

TW-23

S-7

SI-18

S-5

[FIG. 9]

(Continued)

> **NOTE: The following sets of points, are all on the scalp and are used together for the purpose of controlling an opponent's head when grabbing the hair.**

GALL BLADDER # 16, 17, 18: GB-16, GB-17, GB-18 [FIG. 10]
LOCATION: In the scalp, along the curve of the skull, 2 AU either side of the centerline.
ANATOMY: Branches of the frontal and great occipital nerves.

BLADDER # 6, 7, 8: B-6, B-7, B-8 [FIG. 10]
LOCATION: In the scalp, along the curve of the skull, 1 AU either side of the centerline.
ANATOMY: Branches of the frontal and the great occipital nerves.

GALL BLADDER # 8, 9: GB-8, GB-9 [FIG. 11]
LOCATION: In the scalp, along a curved line 1.5 AU supraposterior to the ear. These points are located above and behind the ear on the back quarter of the skull.
ANATOMY: Branches of the great occipital nerve.
METHOD: Rub these points or grab the hair, digging the knuckles into the scalp to control the head.

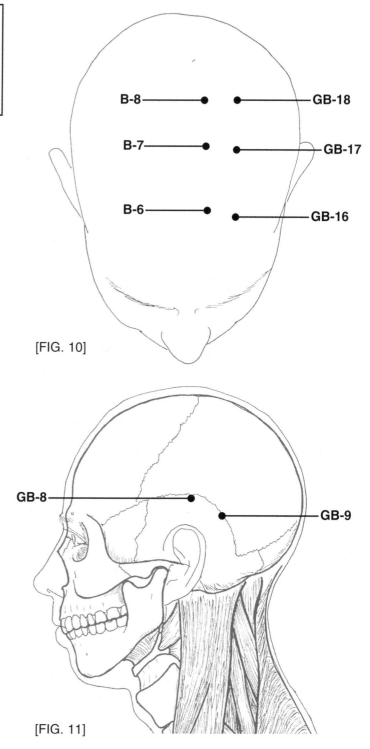

[FIG. 10]

[FIG. 11]

GALL BLADDER # 20: GB-20 [FIG. 12]
LOCATION: In the hollow at the back of neck (between the trapezius and sternocleidomastoid muscles), just below the occipital bone.
ANATOMY: A branch of the lesser occipital nerve.
METHOD: Strike this point from back to front to produce unconsciousness.

BLADDER # 10: B-10 [FIG. 12]
LOCATION: At the base of the skull, 1 AU lateral to the first cervical vertebrae, at the origin of the trapezius muscle.
ANATOMY: The trunk of the great occipital nerve.
METHOD: Strike this point from back to front with a slightly rising motion to knock an opponent to the ground.

> **CAUTION: Never actually strike B-10 in practice.**

SPLEEN # 21: Sp-21 [FIG. 13]
LOCATION: On the mid-axillary line, in the seventh intercostal space. This point can be found on the side of the body, midway between the center of the armpit and the free end of the eleventh (floating) rib.
ANATOMY: The seventh intercostal nerve and the terminal branch of the long thoracic nerve.
METHOD: Strike from the side toward the body-center.

LIVER # 13: Li-13 [FIG. 13]
LOCATION: In the internal and external oblique muscles at the anterior end of the eleventh rib. This point can be located at the free end of the longer of the two floating ribs, at about the place the elbow touches the side of the body.
ANATOMY: The tenth intercostal nerve.
METHOD: Strike this point diagonally upward.

> **CAUTION: Do not strike Li-13 in practice.**

GALL BLADDER # 25: GB-25 [FIG. 13]
LOCATION: At the inferior border of the free end of the twelfth (floating) rib. This point is just at the tip of the smaller of the two floating ribs.
ANATOMY: The 11th intercostal nerve.
METHOD: Strike this point diagonally back to front.

> **CAUTION: Do not strike GB-25 in practice.**

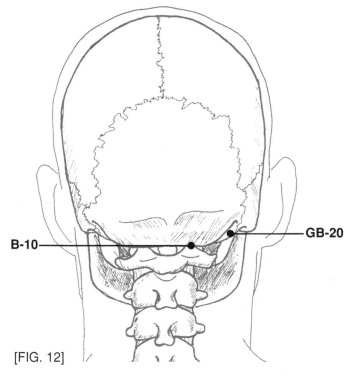

[FIG. 12]

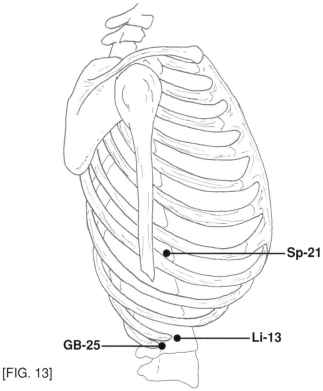

[FIG. 13]

(Continued)

PERICARDIUM # 1: P-1   [FIG. 14]
LOCATION: In the fourth intercostal space, 1 AU supralateral to the nipple. It is just to the outside and above the nipple in the space between the 4th and 5th ribs.
ANATOMY: The muscular branch of the anterior thoracic nerve and the 4th intercostal nerve.
METHOD: Strike on a line toward the center of the back.

STOMACH # 18: S-18   [FIG. 14]
LOCATION: Below the nipple in the fifth intercostal space, at the lower margin of the pectoralis muscle.
ANATOMY: The branch fifth intercostal nerve.
METHOD: Punch this point directly.

CONCEPTION # 17: Co-17   [FIG. 14]
LOCATION: On the sternum, level with the nipples, and just above the articulations of the right and left fifth rib and the sternum.
ANATOMY: A medial anterior cutaneous branch of the fourth intercostal nerve.
METHOD: Strike this point directly.

CAUTION: A blow to the sternum at Co-17 can affect the electrical pattern of the heart resulting in arrhythmia. Do not strike this point in practice.

NOTE: The following two points, Li-14 and GB-24 are in close proximity and are used together.

LIVER # 14: Li-14   [FIG. 14]
LOCATION: At the medial margin of the rib cage at the merging of the sixth and seventh costal cartilage.
ANATOMY: The sixth intercostal nerve.

GALL BLADDER # 24: GB-24   [FIG. 14]
LOCATION: At the medial margin of the rib cage at the merging of the seventh and eighth costal cartilage.
ANATOMY: The seventh intercostal nerve.
METHOD: Strike these points diagonally.

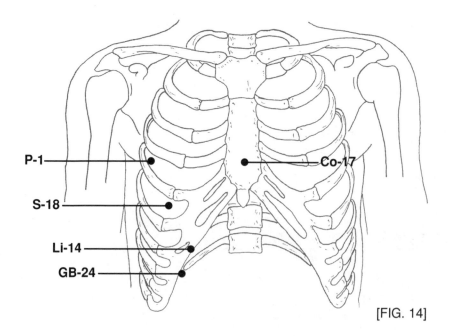

[FIG. 14]

CONCEPTION # 3: Co-3 [FIG. 15]
LOCATION: 4 AU directly below the navel on the median line of the body.
ANATOMY: A branch of the iliohypogastric nerve.

> *NOTE: Co-3 is the alarm point of the bladder meridian. It is also the point at which the three leg yin meridians (kidney, spleen and liver) intersect on the conception meridian.*

The following two points, Li-12 and Sp-12 are in close proximity and are used together.

LIVER # 12: Li-12   [FIG. 15]
LOCATION: Level with the pubic symphysis, 2.5 AU either side of the centerline, in the inguinal groove. It is located in the crease found at the border of the upper thigh and the hips.
ANATOMY: The ilioinguinal nerve, and the anterior branch of the obturator nerve.

SPLEEN #12: Sp-12   [FIG. 15]
LOCATION: Level with the upper border of the pubic symphysis, 3.5 AU lateral to the centerline, in the crease of the leg. It is located just at the outside edge of the femoral artery.
ANATOMY: The femoral nerve.
METHOD: Strike diagonally downward, on a path that moves slightly outward.

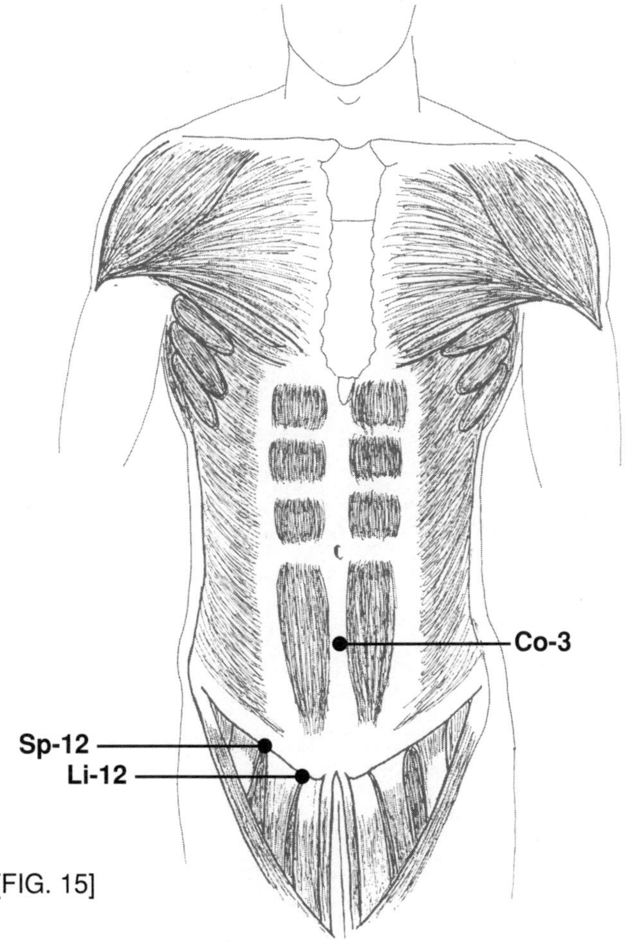

Co-3

Sp-12

Li-12

[FIG. 15]

(Continued)

SPLEEN # 11: Sp-11 [FIG. 16]
LOCATION: Posterior to the sartorius muscle, on the medial aspect of the thigh, about midway between the knee-joint and the groin. This point is located in the middle of the inner thigh.
ANATOMY: The anterior femoral cutaneous nerve and the saphenous nerve.
METHOD: Strike this point to buckle the leg and knock an opponent to the ground.

SPLEEN # 10: Sp-10 [FIG. 16]
LOCATION: At the superior margin of the medial condyle of the femur, in the medial margin of the vastus medialis muscle. This point is on the inner aspect of the leg, about 3 AU proximal to the level of the knee-cap.
ANATOMY: The anterior femoral cutaneous nerve, and a muscular branch of the femoral nerve.
METHOD: Strike diagonally downward to dislocate the knee and/or knock the opponent to the ground.

SPLEEN # 9: Sp-9 [FIG. 16]
LOCATION: In the depression between the posterior margin of the tibia and the gastrocnemius muscle, at the origin of the soleus. This point is on the inner aspect of the knee about 2 AU distal to the knee-cap.
ANATOMY: A cutaneous branch of the saphenous nerve, and the tibial nerve.
METHOD: Strike diagonally upward to dislocate the knee and/or knock the opponent to the ground.

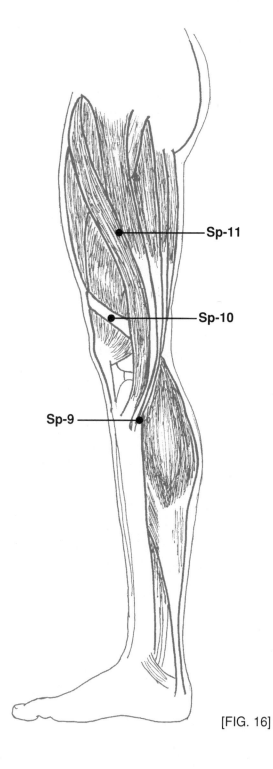

Sp-11

Sp-10

Sp-9

[FIG. 16]

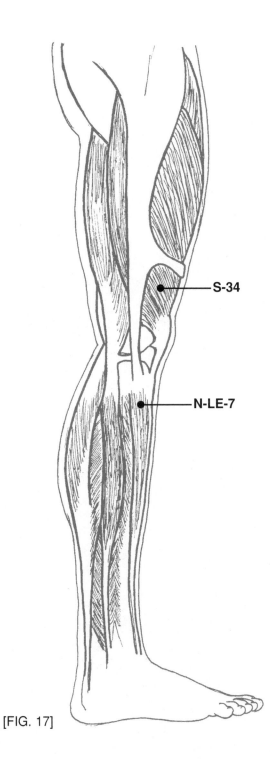

[FIG. 17]

STOMACH # 34: S-34   [FIG. 17]
LOCATION: On the lateral aspect of the thigh in the vastus lateralis muscle, at the border of the vastus medialis muscle. This point is about 3 AU proximal to the knee-cap on the outside of the thigh.
ANATOMY: This point is situated directly on the lateral femoral cutaneous nerve.
METHOD: Strike diagonally downward to dislocate the knee and/or knock the opponent to the ground.

N-LE-7: Extraordinary Point   [FIG. 17]
LOCATION: About 3 AU below the knee lateral to the tibia in the tibialis anterior muscle.
ANATOMY: The lateral cutaneous nerve of the calf, a cutaneous branch of the saphenous nerve and the deep peroneal nerve.
METHOD: Strike diagonally upward to dislocate the knee and/or knock the opponent to the ground.

(Continued)

GALL BLADDER # 41: GB-41   [FIG. 18]

LOCATION: In the depression just in front of the merging of the fourth and fifth metatarsal bones. It is located just in front of the bulge on the top of the foot where the bones of the fourth and fifth toes connect.

ANATOMY: The dorsal digital nerve of the fourth metatarsus.

METHOD: Stomp or grind on this point with a front to back motion.

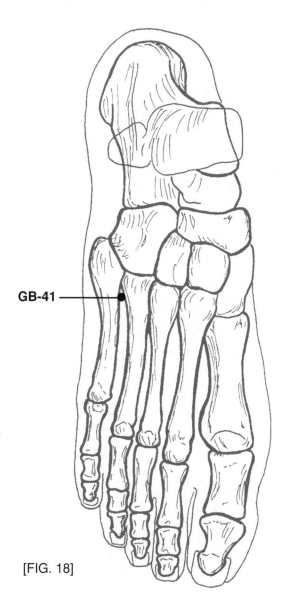

GB-41

[FIG. 18]

BIBLIOGRAPHY & SOURCES FOR CHAPTER 3

ACADEMY OF TRADITIONAL CHINESE MEDICINE
An Outline of Chinese Acupuncture
Chan's Corporation
Monterey Park, CA, 1983

BEIJING COLLEGE OF TRADITIONAL CHINESE MEDICINE et. al
Essentials of Chinese Acupuncture
Pergamon Press Ltd.
Elmsford, New York, 1981

GRANT, J. C. Boileau
Grant's Atlas of Anatomy, 6th ed.
The Williams and Wilkins Co.
Baltimore, MD, 1972

GUYTON, Arthur C., M.D.
Text Book of Medical Physiology, 7th ed.
W. B. Saunders, Co.
Philadelphia, 1986

HOLLINSHEAD, W. Henry, Ph.D.
Anatomy for Surgeons: Volume 1
The Head and the Neck, 2nd ed.
Harper & Row, Publishers, Inc.
Hagerstown, MD 1968

NETTER, Frank H., M.D.
Atlas of Human Anatomy
CIBA-GEIGY Ltd.
Basle, Switzerland, 1989

SHANDONG MEDICAL COLLEGE & SHANDONG COLLEGE OF TRADITIONAL CHINESE MEDICINE
Anatomical Atlas of Chinese Acupuncture Points
Pergamon Press for
Shandong Science and Technology Press
Elmsford, New York, 1982

SHANGHAI COLLEGE OF TRADITIONAL MEDICINE
Acupuncture: A Comprehensive Text
tr. John O'Connor & Dan Bensky
Eastland Press
Seattle, WA, 1981

WILSON-PAUWELS, AKESSON, STEWART
Cranial Nerves: Anatomy and Clinical Comments
B. C. Decker, Inc.
Philadelphia, PA, 1988

When it snows in Pennsylvania, "It snows" Allen B. Dillman and George A. Dillman with their karate snowman, early 1980's

BASIC TUITÉ-WAZA

To be able to use the methods of tuité-jitsu successfully in self-defense, one must first have a working knowledge of the basic joint manipulations of the art. In this chapter fundamental techniques are demonstrated. It is important that the reader pay particular attention to the way in which the opponent's joint is being twisted, and not how the defender applies the technique. As is evident in the next chapter, each manipulation can be acquired in many different ways. For example, what makes a palm turn (see page 69) a palm turn is not which hand the defender uses, but what happens to the attacker.

Also, it is important to pay attention to the concept of compound manipulation. Different basic techniques can be combined — or compounded — to involve more joints. The results can be extremely painful, but the reader needs to be aware that compound techniques can take longer to apply because they require "taking up the slack" in multiple joints.

FINGER LOCKING

It is possible to apply a finger lock by following this simple rule: bend and twist. The most simple finger lock is done by bending the finger back at the knuckle (hyper-extension) and then twisting.

Locking the thumb is done differently because the thumb is structured differently. To lock the thumb, bend it at the tip, then rotate outwards.

Acupuncture meridians begin or end at the tip of each finger. Manipulating the fingers affects the energy flow in these meridians. When the thumb is locked, the lung meridian is affected. Locking the index finger affects large intestine. The middle finger affects pericardium, and the fourth finger affects triple warmer. The little finger affects heart and small intestine.

BASIC METHOD 1:

1. Grasp your training partner's right index finger with your right hand.

2. With a turn of your wrist, use two-way action to bend his finger back.

3. As his finger bends back, twist it toward the outside with a counter-clockwise motion.

NOTE: Be sure to practice all basic methods on both your right and left sides.

(Continued)

BASIC METHOD 2:

4. With your left hand, grasp your training partner's right little and ring fingers.

5. With a turn of your wrist, use two-way action to bend his fingers back.

6. As his fingers bend backward, twist them inward with a clockwise rotation.

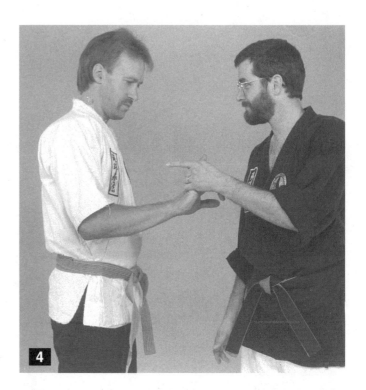

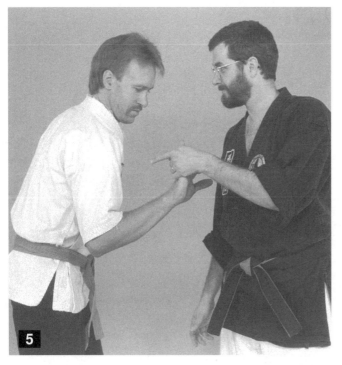

BASIC METHOD 3:

1. With your left hand grasp your training partner's right index finger so that it points downward (palm up or supine).

2. Lift upward and torque his finger with two-way action.

3. Twist the index finger inward with a clockwise rotation.

> **NOTE: This produces a compound lock, because as you lift upward, his arm straightens and locks at the elbow.**

(Continued)

BASIC METHOD 4:

4. Grasp your training partner's right hand with your left hand, holding it palm up (supine).

5. With your right hand, bend his thumb at both the first and second joints.

6. Twist his bent thumb diagonally backward rotating against the joint.

PALM TURN

Bend the opponent's wrist backward (dorsiflexion) and turn the back of the hand inward (medial rotation) by pressure against the little finger (fifth digit). A key to this technique is to squeeze the little finger behind the ring finger (fourth digit).

Applying a palm turn activates the heart and small intestine meridians. Follow-up attacks can be aimed to points on these meridians: heart or small intestine (attack yin/yang), large intestine or lung (cycle of destruction), bladder (diurnal cycle).

BASIC METHOD:

1. With your training partner's right hand held palm out, fingers pointing up, grasp his wrist with your left hand, place your right palm against his fingers and squeeze his little finger behind the ring finger.

2. Rotate inward against his little finger, twisting in a clockwise motion.

WRIST REVERSAL

Bend the opponent's hand toward his body (palmar flexion with forearm supination). Then press to bend his arm (elbow flexion), and turn his palm outward (lateral rotation resulting in hyper-supination of the forearm) by pressure against the back of the hand proximal to the knuckle of the ring finger (fourth digit).

When grabbing the opponent's hand, your fingers will dig into the meat of the thumb at L-10 and your thumb presses on TW-3. Follow-up attacks can be aimed to the lung meridian, triple warmer meridian, or any of the following: large intestine (cycle of destruction relative to triple warmer and yin/yang as well as diurnal cycle relative to lung), liver (cycle of destruction relative to lung), or gall bladder (cycle of destruction relative to lung and diurnal cycle relative to triple warmer).

BASIC METHOD:

1. Grasp your training partner's right hand with your left hand, your fingers on the meat of his thumb, and your thumb on the back of his hand in the hollow between the bones of the fourth and fifth fingers (fourth and fifth metacarpals).

2. Bend his wrist back and rotate his hand outward (counter-clockwise from your perspective).

3-4. Press his hand past the outside of his right shoulder.

NOTE: This technique is usually done applying pressure with both of your hands (Fig. 3 & 4), but can also be applied with just one hand (Fig. 1 & 2).

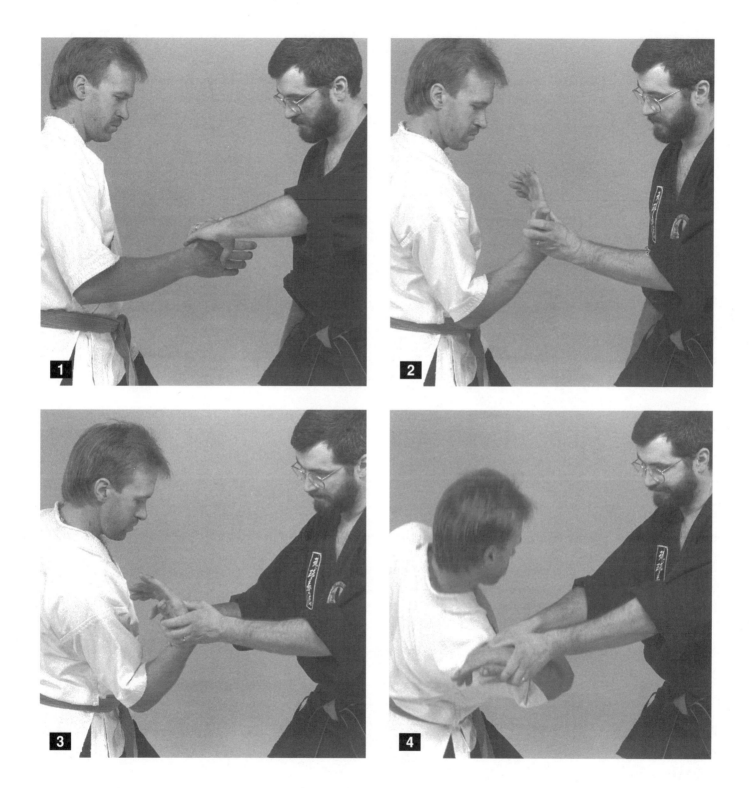

(Continued)

EXTENSION:

5. Apply a wrist reversal against his right hand with your left hand (as explained above).

6. Step in toward the opponent and strike downward with a "chicken beak" strike (see the appendix for information on this hand formation). Since the wrist reversal is done with pressure on TW-3, continue your attack on that meridian by striking TW-17 under his ear.

NOTE: This technique is based on a movement from the kata Goseishi (called Gojushi-ho in Japanese).

WRIST TURN/PRESS

Turn the opponent's hand so that his palm faces to the side, with the thumb down, and the elbow turns out (pronation of the forearm, leading to abduction of the shoulder). Bend the wrist slightly so that the angle between the palm and the forearm is about 130 degrees (palmar flexion). Apply pressure upward at the knuckle of the index finger and downward at the little finger side of the wrist (ulnar deviation). A key to this technique is to have a slight bend in the elbow (flexion) so that the angles of the elbow and the wrist form the shape of an "S". (For this reason, this manipulation is sometimes called an S-lock.)

When applying this technique, press upward in the web of the attacker's thumb at LI-4 and downward on the wrist at SI-6. Finishing moves can follow the meridians, attacking again to the large intestine or small intestine meridians (attacking large intestine also creates a cycle of destruction relative to small intestine). You may also attack stomach (diurnal cycle relative to large intestine), lung (yin/yang relative to large intestine and cycle of destruction from small intestine), either liver or gall bladder (cycle of destruction relative to large intestine) or bladder (diurnal cycle of small intestine).

BASIC METHOD:

1. Grab your training partner's right hand with your right hand (your thumb in the web of his thumb and your fingers wrapped around the little finger side) and rotate his hand inward so that his thumb is down and his palm faces to your left. Lay your left forearm across his right forearm, and lightly grab his wrist.

2. Press upward against the bone of his index finger (second metacarpal) with a twisting action of your right hand, and press downward on his forearm with your left arm.

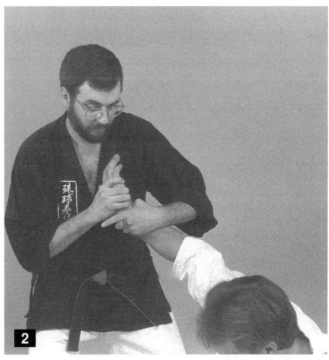

(Continued)

COMPOUNDING THE LOCK

1-3. To compound the wrist turn/press, grasp his fingers with your left hand and bend his little finger behind his fourth finger. From your point of view, his little finger is bent to the right, his wrist is bent to the left and his elbow to the right.

FOREARM TURN

Turn the opponent's hand thumb down, toward the outside (hyper-supination of the forearm). This movement is similar to a wrist reversal, but the wrist is not bent.

When grabbing the opponent's hand, your fingers will dig into the meat of the thumb at L-10 and your thumb presses on TW-3. Follow-up attacks can be aimed to the lung meridian, triple warmer meridian, or any of the following: large intestine (cycle of destruction relative to triple warmer and yin/yang as well as diurnal cycle relative to lung), liver (cycle of destruction relative to lung), or gall bladder (cycle of destruction relative to lung and diurnal cycle relative to triple warmer).

BASIC METHOD:

1. Your training partner grabs your left wrist with his right hand.

2-3. Circle your left hand inward so that your palm faces up.

4. Reach across with your right hand, and grab your training partner's right hand from underneath, grasping the meat of his thumb and peeling his hand off your wrist.

5. With your left hand, press against the back of his hand just below the knuckle of the fourth finger (proximal and slightly lateral to the fourth metacarpalphalangeal joint) as you pull against his thumb with your right hand.

6. Turn his hand sharply to the side (hyper-supination of the forearm) with a counter-clockwise rotation.

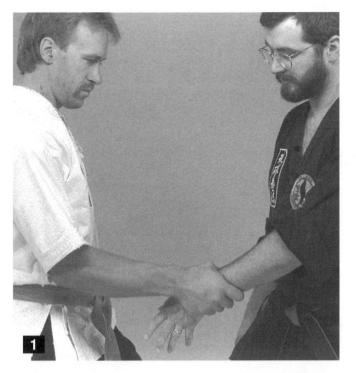

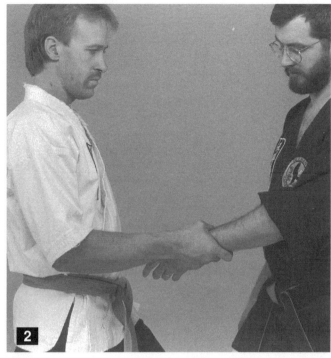

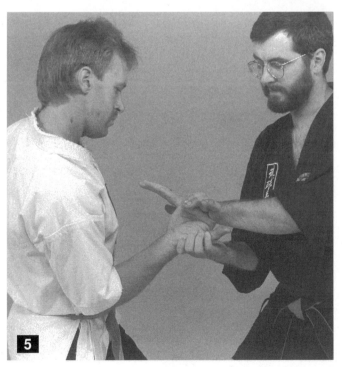

ELBOW LOCK

Straighten the opponent's arm and apply pressure to the back of the elbow (elbow hyper-extension). The opponent's arm is released by attacking either TW-11 or TW-12, and pressure is maintained on these points. Follow-up techniques can be directed to triple warmer, gall bladder (diurnal cycle), pericardium (yin/yang), lung or large intestine (cycle of destruction).

BASIC METHOD 1:

1. Grasp your training partner's left hand at the wrist with your left hand and turn his hand so his thumb faces down and his elbow points to the side.

2. With the extended knuckle of the middle finger of your right hand press just above the point of his elbow at TW-11.

3-5. With an up and down motion stimulate the pressure point to release the elbow and lock the arm.

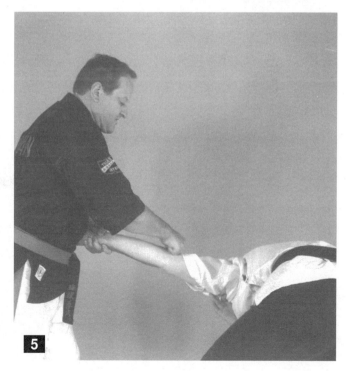

(Continued)

BASIC METHOD 2:

1-4. Holding your training partner's left arm with your left hand (as in the previous exercise), strike the back of his arm mid-triceps at TW-12 to release his elbow and lock out his arm.

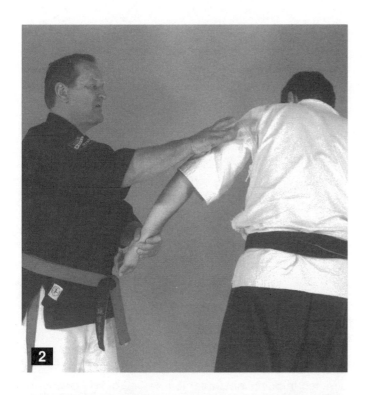

CHICKEN WINGS (4)

There are four types of chicken wings. What is common to them all is that the arm is bent at both the wrist and elbow, and pressure is applied against the hand as if pulling it to the elbow.

A. Bend the opponent's hand so his palm faces back and his fingers point toward his shoulder (elbow flexion, forearm supination and palmar flexion of the wrist). As the hand is squeezed back toward the elbow, pressure is applied below the knuckle of the fourth finger.

Pressure at the fourth finger affects triple warmer. Follow-up may be directed against the triple warmer, pericardium (yin/yang), gall bladder (diurnal cycle), lung or large intestine (cycle of destruction) meridians.

B. Bend the opponent's hand so his palm faces back and his fingers point downward (elbow flexion, forearm pronation and palmar flexion of the wrist). As the hand is squeezed back toward the elbow, pressure is applied below the knuckle of the index finger.

The large intestine meridian begins at the tip of the index finger. Therefore, continuation of the attack should be directed to points on the large intestine, lung (yin/yang), stomach (diurnal cycle), liver or gall bladder (cycle of destruction) meridians.

C. Bend the opponent's hand so his palm faces outward and his fingers point up (elbow flexion, forearm pronation and dorsiflexion of the wrist). As the hand is squeezed back toward the elbow, pressure is applied against the little finger.

Pressure on the little finger stimulates heart and small intestine so that points on either meridian may be used for follow-up. Also, you may attack the bladder meridian to follow the diurnal cycle relative to small intestine, and either the large intestine or lung meridians to use the cycle of destruction.

D. Bend the opponent's hand so his palm faces outward and his fingers point down (elbow flexion, forearm supination and dorsiflexion of the wrist). As the hand is squeezed back toward the elbow, pressure is applied against the index finger.

The large intestine meridian begins at the tip of the index finger. Continuation of the attack should be directed to points on the large intestine, lung (yin/yang), stomach (diurnal cycle), liver or gall bladder (cycle of destruction) meridians.

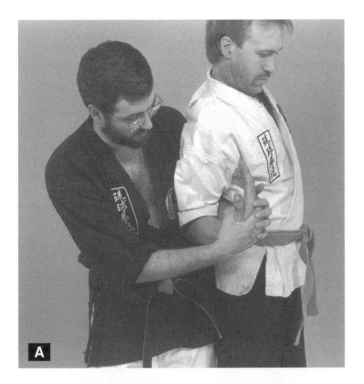

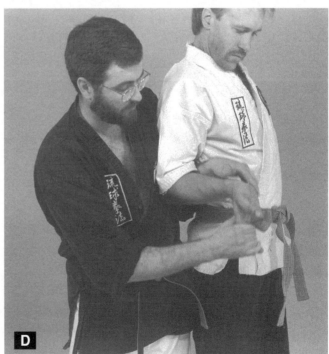

LATERAL PALM TURN

With his arm bent and elbow pointing to the side, bend the opponent's hand back at the wrist and point his little finger at his chest (shoulder abduction, elbow flexion, forearm pronation and dorsiflexion of the wrist). Apply pressure back toward the elbow and down toward the ground (resulting in hyper-pronation of the forearm, and hyper-dorsiflexion of the wrist).

Applying a lateral palm turn activates the heart and small intestine meridians. Follow-up attacks can be aimed to points on these meridians: heart or small intestine (attack yin/yang), large intestine or lung (cycle of destruction), bladder (diurnal cycle).

BASIC METHOD:

1. As your training partner holds his left arm level with the ground, his palm facing you, meet his palm with your left hand, turning his little finger behind his ring finger.
2. Apply downward pressure on his little finger to start his body moving and confuse his joints.
3. Thread your right arm under his elbow and over his hand, to grasp him by the fingers.
4. Pull his hand tightly, as if trying to tuck his little finger into his armpit. This position may be used as a come-along.
5. Press downward on the little finger of your partner's captured hand to drop him violently to the ground.

CAUTION: Use restraint as this technique puts tremendous pressure on the fingers and wrist.

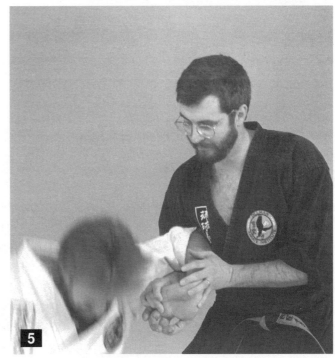

STANDING PALM TURN

With the opponent's forearm held vertically at his side, bend his hand so that the palm faces down and the fingers point toward his body (internal rotation of the shoulder, flexion of the elbow, pronation of the forearm and dorsiflexion of the wrist). Apply pressure by lifting against the fingers, and rotating the hand toward the rear (resulting in hyper-flexion of the wrist and hyper-pronation of the forearm).

This technique puts pressure especially against the little finger, stimulating heart and small intestine meridians. Continue with attacks to points on heart or small intestine (yin/yang in relation to each other), bladder (diurnal cycle relative to small intestine), large intestine or lung (cycle of destruction).

BASIC METHOD:

1. As your training partner reaches around your body from behind, grasp his right hand with your left hand, on the little finger side of his palm.

2. Step back and slip under his arm, as you grasp his right hand from below with your right hand, squeezing his little finger behind his ring finger.

3. Slide your left hand up his forearm to control his elbow, as you lift and turn his hand backward.

NOTE: Photo A shows a detail of the pressure against the hand.

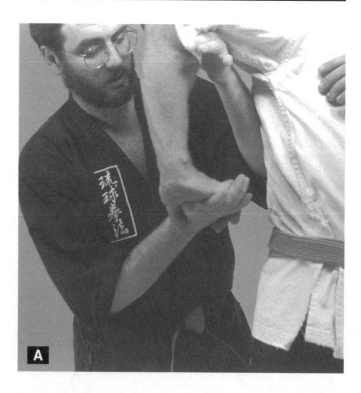

A

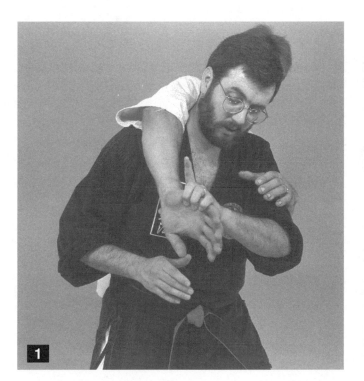

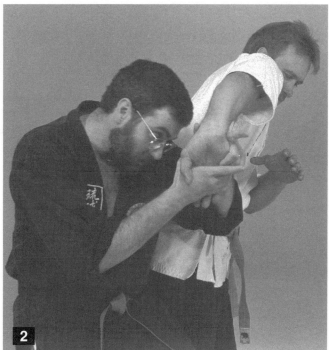

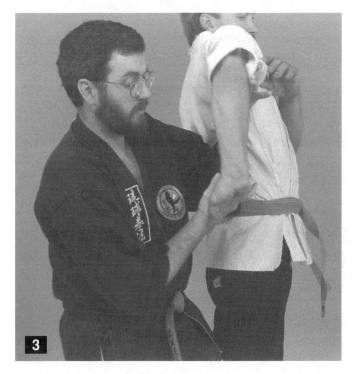

BACK SHOULDER LOCK

With the opponent's elbow bent, hand pointing down, bring his arm behind his back (a combination of hyper-extension and internal rotation of the shoulder). Lever the arm upward at the wrist and downward at the elbow (resulting in internal hyper-rotation of the shoulder).

The downward pressure at the elbow is directed against H-2. Follow-up attacks can be aimed to points on the heart, small intestine (yin/yang and diurnal cycle), lung or large intestine (cycle of destruction).

BASIC METHOD:

1. Grasp your training partner's wrist with your left hand.

2. Strike the inside of his arm with your right hand at H-2. This causes his elbow to bend and his arm to rotate so his forearm points downward.

3-4. Thread your left arm under his right wrist and over his elbow at H-2.

5. Apply pressure down on H-2 with your hand, and up at his wrist with your elbow (two-way action) to lock your opponent's shoulder.

(Continued)

COMPOUNDING THE LOCK:

A. To compound this technique, grab your training partner's hair and pull his head back toward his locked elbow. This locks the spine and increases the pressure against the shoulder.

CAUTION: Use restraint as this technique can injure the neck (whiplash effect)

FRONT SHOULDER LOCK

With the opponent's arm bent in front (shoulder extension, and elbow flexion), lift inward against the elbow and press downward against the wrist (resulting in external hyper-rotation of the shoulder).

The inward pressure is applied at LI-11. Continuation of the attack should be directed to points on the large intestine, lung (yin/yang), stomach (diurnal cycle), liver or gall bladder (cycle of destruction).

BASIC METHOD:

1. Have your training partner stand with his right hand held about shoulder height, and his elbow bent about 90 degrees.

2. Place your left wrist on the inside of his right wrist, and your right wrist on the outside of his forearm near the elbow (at LI-11).

3. Press down on his wrist, while drawing his elbow up and in to lock his shoulder.

NOTE: In this exercise you can grab him at the wrist and elbow, or work on your sticking hands skills (muchimi) as shown.

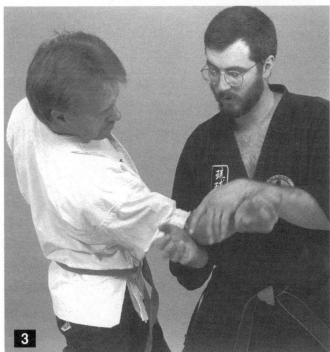

(Continued)

95

COMPOUNDING THE LOCK:

A-B. To compound the lock, apply a wrist reversal with your left hand against your training partner's right wrist as you pull his elbow inward to execute the shoulder lock.

NOTE: To increase the severity of the technique, grasp at the elbow with your right hand, digging your fingers into LI-10 on the outside of the arm, and the tip of your thumb into H-2 on the inside of the arm just above the elbow.

HEAD TURN

Basic head turning is done by grasping the opponent's hair with one hand at the opposite rear quadrant of his head and pushing or striking the front quadrant with the other hand. Use two-way action, pulling the back of his head forward and pushing the front of his head back.

Grasping on the back side of the head stimulates the gall bladder meridian. Pressure on the jaw is against the stomach meridian. Follow-up attacks may be aimed at gall bladder, stomach, spleen (cycle of destruction relative to gall bladder, and yin/yang relative to stomach), liver (yin/yang in relation to gall bladder), kidney or bladder (cycle of destruction from stomach).

BASIC METHOD:

1. With your left hand, grasp your training partner by the hair on the back of his head, on the left side. With your right hand, press on the outer edge of his jaw on the right side of his face.

2-6. Using two-way action, spin him by his head, circling back and up with your right hand, and pulling around and down with your left.

CAUTION: Always perform this technique slowly and smoothly to prevent neck injury. In particular, never jerk a training partner's head.

TUITÉ PROGRESSIONS

Tuité progressions are a method of moving from one joint technique to another. As each technique is applied, the opponent will try to squirm out. He will bend his elbow, turn his shoulder, etc. These movements of resistance against one technique, actually make it easy to apply the next technique. A tuité progression can be used in two ways.

First, you may use it responsively. If you are attempting to apply a technique and the opponent resists, simply follow the direction of his resistance and progress to a different technique.

Second, you may use this method pro-actively. In this case you intentionally apply one technique knowing that the attacker will resist, and intending then to capitalize on his natural body reflexes. The pro-active approach also capitalizes on the principle of creating confusion. Each technique moves the attacker's body in a particular manner, making it impossible for him to resist when you apply a different technique which moves his body in a completely different direction.

EXAMPLE

1. Your training partner grabs your lapel with his left hand.

2-3. Step back slightly and apply a wrist turn/press.

NOTE: This is an example of a pro-active tuité progression.

(Continued)

4. Immediately step forward into a horse stance, locking his arm against your right leg with pressure on his elbow using your right elbow.

5-6. Bend his arm at wrist and elbow and apply upward pressure (a "standing" chicken wing) lifting him to his feet.

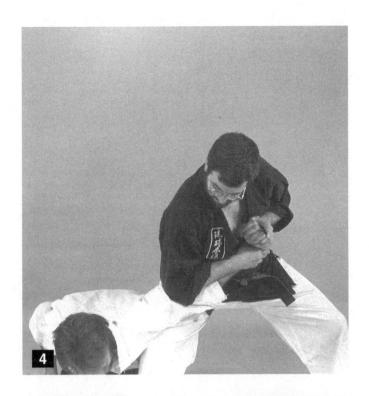

Tuité-jitsu is an ideal art for young people because, unlike kicking and punching methods, tuité-waza are suitable for dealing with schoolyard bullies without causing serious harm.

TUITÉ SELF-DEFENSE AGAINST SIMPLE ASSAULTS

The point of Ryukyu kempo training is to become equipped to defend oneself. Therefore, a good portion of training must be devoted to practicing responses to various types of attacks. However, if one simply trains response "X" to attack "Y", it will be impossible to use these techniques in a real encounter, unless one is attacked exactly as it is done in class. For this reason it is important to understand the principles which are being employed. For this reason, the reader is urged to be familiar with the 9 principles of tuité discussed in chapter two.

TECHNIQUE # 1

1. An attacker threatens with his right fist.

2. Reach up with your left hand and seize his arm, pressing the fingertips into point H-6 to weaken his wrist.

3-4. Lay your right hand against point TW-3 on the back of the opponent's fist (the combination of the pressure points H-6 and TW-3 will cause his fist to weaken and his wrist to buckle), and press the point back toward the outside of the attacker's right shoulder (a basic wrist reversal).

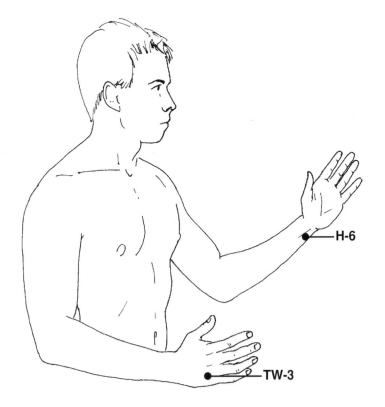

NOTE: Gichin Funakoshi, wrote a famous proverb, "Karate-ni sente nashi." This translates to, "Karate has no first attack," and means, "In karate one does not make the first aggressive move." This, does not mean, however, that one should wait until an assailant has actually made an attack. Self-defense begins before the first physical technique is thrown. In this example, tuité-waza is used at the first sign of a threat, to preclude any serious attack. This underscores one of the benefits of tuité-jitsu: these techniques can be administered at a low intensity which does not cause serious physical injury.

(Continued)

TECHNIQUE # 1 (Continued)

5-6. As the opponent begins to fold turn his wrist toward your left side (complex torque), and take him to the ground.

Option: at any time during this movement, your opponent can be struck on a Kyusho pressure point.

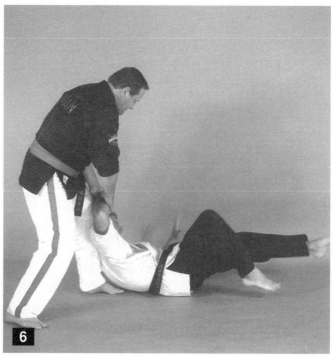

TECHNIQUE # 2

This technique illustrates how effective tuité can be for anyone. The defender, a 10 year old, easily controls her much stronger adult attacker.

NOTE: To sprain the finger creates intense pain and shock, thereby allowing you to escape without being pursued. However, it is a serious thing to injure another person in this manner, and should only be done if it is absolutely necessary to protect yourself from bodily harm.

1. An assailant has placed his right hand on your left shoulder, an unwanted touch.

2. Lay your left arm across the middle of his forearm on SI-7, pressing toward your own centerline.

3-4. With your right hand, grasp his little finger and bend it back, while maintaining inward pressure on his forearm.

5. As you bend his finger, press in toward your shoulder, using your body to create a base. If the situation warrants, you may need to step forward and turn 45 degrees inward to sprain the attacker's little finger, giving you the chance to run away.

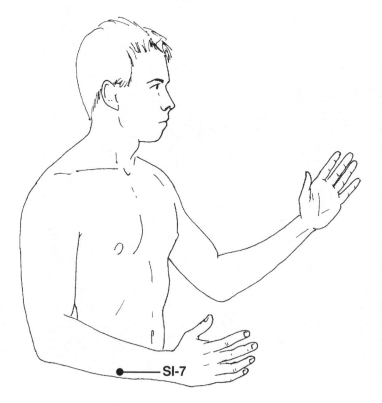

SI-7

TECHNIQUE # 3

1. An attacker reaches with his right hand to grab or shove.

2-3. Intercept his right hand with your left hand (thumb down) pressing your palm against his fingers. At the same time, grasp his wrist with your right hand, pressing your thumb into H-6 and rolling your fingertips across SI-6.

H-6 and SI-6 are used because both the heart and small intestine meridians follow the little finger.

4. Using your right hand, pull his wrist toward your body, while twisting against the little finger (complex torque) to drop the opponent.

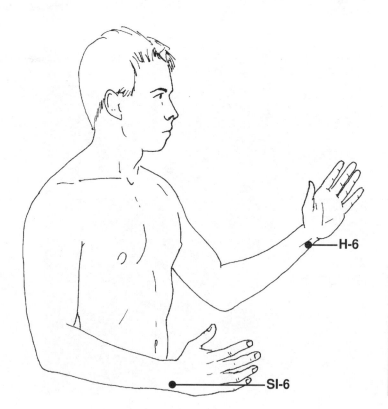

H-6

SI-6

NOTE: As the final pressure is applied, the opponent's left arm swings wildly backward and away. This means that the opponent is helpless to fight back even using his free hand. This reaction is called the crossed-extensor reflex and is a common result of the application of tuité-waza.

(Continued)

TECHNIQUE # 3 (Continued)

A-B. In close-up it is possible to see an important detail in the palm turn: the opponent's little finger is rolled back behind the ring finger. This action undermines the mechanical structure of the hand and disrupts the proper flow of ki through the arm.

TECHNIQUE # 4

1. An attacker reaches with his right hand to grab or shove.

2-3.   At the same time, grasp his wrist with your left hand. Reach across with your right hand (thumb down) and intercept his hand pressing your fingers against his fingers.

4. Using your left hand, pull his wrist toward you, while pressing his fingers back with your right hand (two-way action).

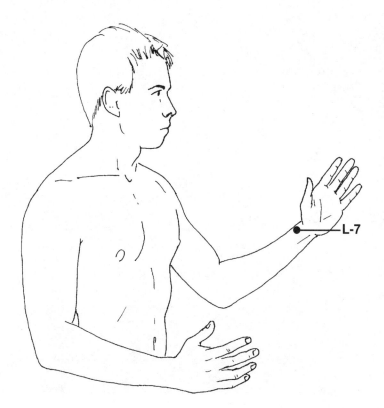

L-7

*NOTE: The heart and small intestine meridians have the elemental value "fire" and the lung meridian is of the element "metal." In the cycle of destruction, "fire" melts "metal." This means that manipulating the little finger makes the lung point vulnerable to attack.   For more information on the "Cycle of destruction" refer to our book **Advanced Pressure Point Fighting of RYUKYU KEMPO**, pages 56-58.*

(Continued)

TECHNIQUE # 4 (Continued)

5-6. Twist against the little finger (complex torque) with your right hand while rolling across wrist point L-7 with the thumb of your left hand to drop the opponent.

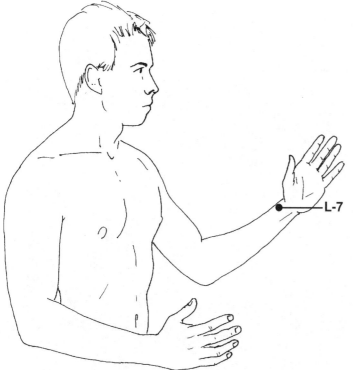

L-7

TECHNIQUE # 5

1. An attacker reaches with his right hand to grab or shove.

2-3. Intercept his right hand with the back of your left hand, pressing it against his fingers. At the same time, grasp his wrist with your right hand, pressing your thumb into H-6 and rolling your fingertips across SI-6.

4. Using your right hand, pull his wrist toward you, while pressing his fingers back with your left hand (two-way action).

5. Twist against the little finger (complex torque) to drop the opponent.

1

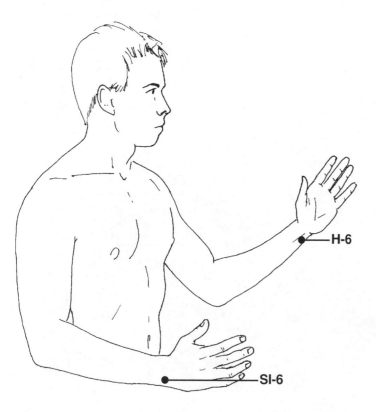

H-6

SI-6

NOTE: This technique is similar to technique # 3 above, different only in that the back of the left hand, instead of the palm, is used to apply the pressure.

TECHNIQUE # 6

1. An attacker reaches with his right hand to grab or shove.

2. Using your right hand, trap the opponent's hand to the left side of your chest.

3. Grasp his little finger with your right hand, pulling it across his ring finger, and cut with your left arm across SI-7 on his forearm.

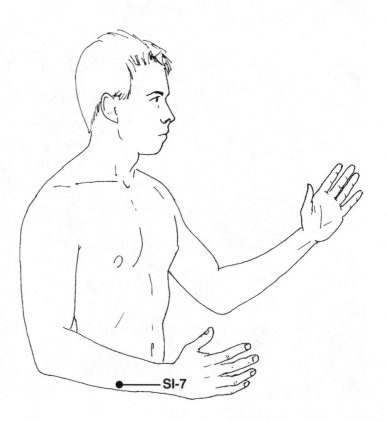

(Continued)

TECHNIQUE # 6 (Continued)

4-5. Turn to your right, allowing your body motion to press and twist the opponent's hand to lock and control him.

A-D. In close-up you can clearly see the action of lifting the opponent's little finger, and the way in which the left hand cuts across the forearm point SI-7.

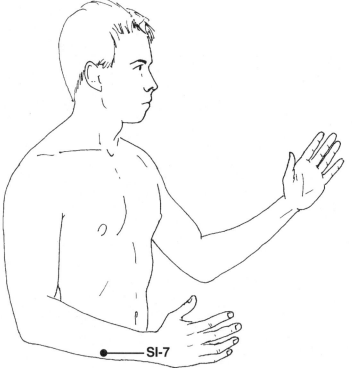

TECHNIQUE # 7

1. An attacker reaches with his right hand to grab or shove.

2. Allow him to grab your left forearm.

3-4. With your right hand, grasp the attacker's wrist on pressure points H-6 and L-8.

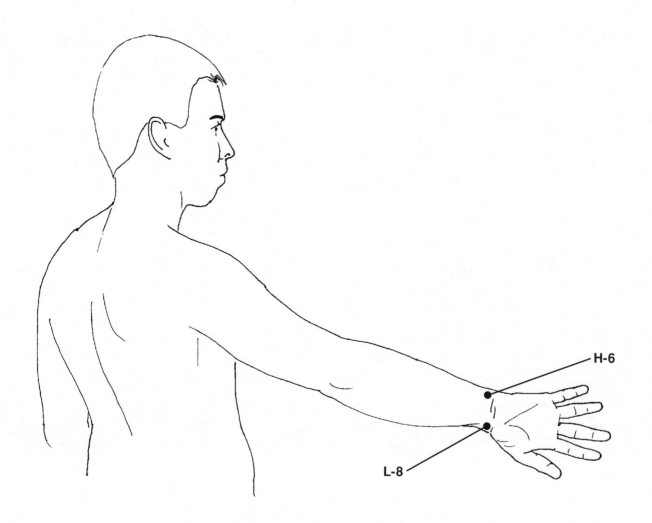

(Continued)

127

TECHNIQUE # 7 (Continued)

5. Turn to your right, and swing your elbow forward, using your forearm to press and twist your opponent's hand to apply a palm turn.

6. The application of the palm turn exposes the back of the attacker's head. As you continue to turn and apply pressure against his hand, strike with your elbow to B-10 at the base of the opponent's skull ("Attack a joint to strike a point").

> **NOTE: The energy flows through the body from the heart meridian to the small intestine meridian, from the small intestine meridian to the bladder meridian. This is part of the diurnal cycle of ki, and explains why the palm turn exposes and "sets up" a bladder point for attack. The diurnal cycle is explained in our book *Advanced Pressure Point Fighting of RYUKYU KEMPO,* pages 54-55.**

> **CAUTION: Never strike B-10 in practice.**

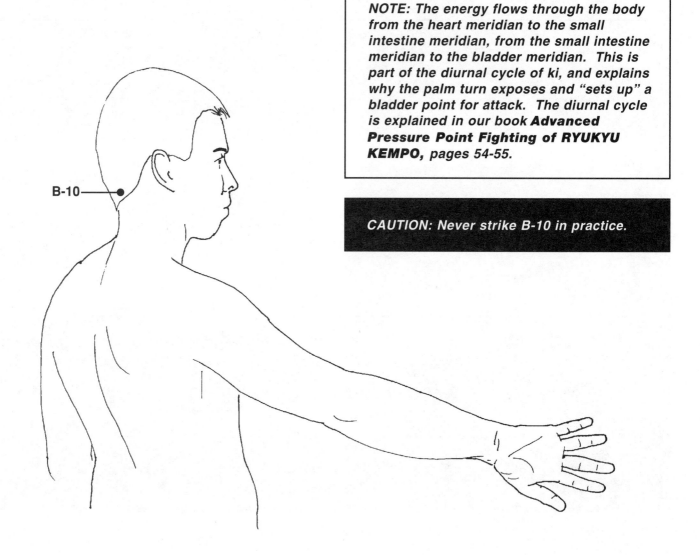

B-10

TECHNIQUE # 8

CAUTION: In other techniques it is easy to instantly release the hold if your partner is in danger of injury. However, this technique wraps the arm so tightly that he can be injured before you are aware. For this reason, practice with extreme care.

1. An attacker reaches with his right hand to grab or shove.

2. Reach with your left hand (thumb down) and intercept his hand pressing your palm against his fingers.

3-4. Thread your right arm over his right forearm, then under your left arm, so your arms form an X.

5. Turn to your right and draw your hands toward your center.

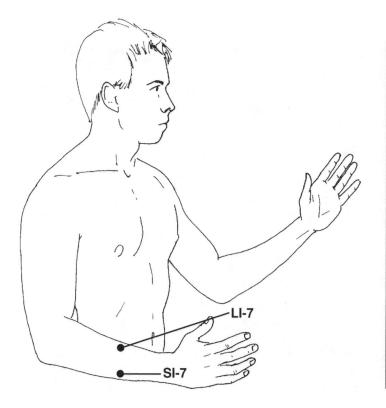

LI-7

SI-7

3

(Continued)

TECHNIQUE # 8 (Continued)

A-F. In close-up the details of this technique become more clear.

[A] Your left hand intercepts your opponent's right hand, pressing against his fingers with your palm.

[B-C] As your right arm rolls over your opponent's forearm, you first cut across point LI-7 on the radial side of the arm, and then across SI-7 on the ulnar side. This action can be compared to the movement of bowing a violin.

[D-E] When you thread your right arm under your left, you must be careful to draw your right elbow back close to your body to "take up the slack" on your opponent's joint.

[F] Once the opponent is trapped, you may move forward and turn your body to apply pressure. (In this technique you are working to your mechanical advantage, drawing your arms close to your chest, and using your whole body to put pressure on the attacker's wrist.)

TECHNIQUE # 9

1. An attacker has grabbed your left forearm with his right hand (thumb up).

2. Bend your elbow and draw your left hand toward the base of your sternum. (This action creates a mechanical advantage for you in that you draw into your strength, and work against the weakest part of his grip: the thumb and index finger).

3. Do not try to pull out of his grip. Instead, step forward slightly and strike his forearm at LI-7 with your elbow. This will release his hold.

4. With your freed left hand, strike S-9 on the left side of the opponent's neck.

When a person grabs you anywhere on the arm, he cannot prevent you from bending your own elbow. This is the basis for all defenses against such attacks.

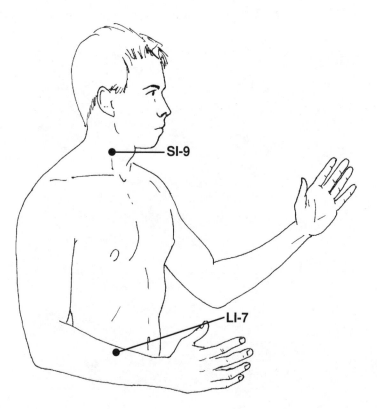

NOTE: Attacking on the large intestine meridian then the stomach meridian follows the diurnal cycle of ki. Refer to **Advanced Pressure Point Fighting of RYUKYU KEMPO,** *pages 54-55.*

TECHNIQUE # 10

1. An attacker has grabbed your left forearm with his left hand.

2. Bend your left elbow and draw your fist toward the base of your sternum. Do not struggle with your adversary. If his grip is so strong that you cannot pull him to you, then slide forward and bend your elbow that way.

3-5. Roll your arm in a counter-clockwise (from your viewpoint) circle to release his grasp, and grab his wrist in turn, squeezing on points H-6 and L-8.

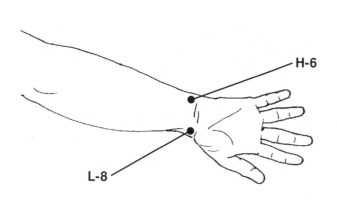

(Continued)

TECHNIQUE # 10 (Continued)

6-8. Holding tightly with your left hand, bend his wrist toward his forearm, pressing against "extraordinary" point M-UE-24 and drive him over.

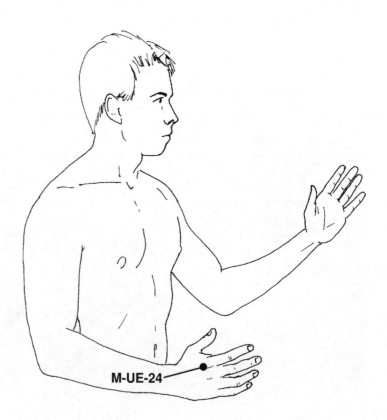

M-UE-24

TECHNIQUE # 11

1. An attacker has grabbed both of your arms.

2. Bend your left arm and roll your elbow over your opponent's forearm. At the same time, trap his right hand to your left forearm using your right hand.

3. Step back into a side-horse stance to stretch and unbalance the attacker.

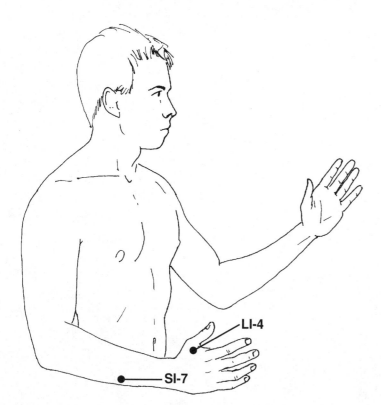

LI-4

SI-7

NOTE: Tuité-jitsu is an ideal art for young people because, unlike kicking and punching methods, tuité-waza are suitable for dealing with schoolyard bullies without causing serious harm.

(Continued)

TECHNIQUE # 11 (Continued)

4-5. With your right hand press upward against LI-4 in the web of the thumb on your opponent's right hand, and press down with your elbow on SI-7, applying the basic tuité-waza "wrist turn/press".

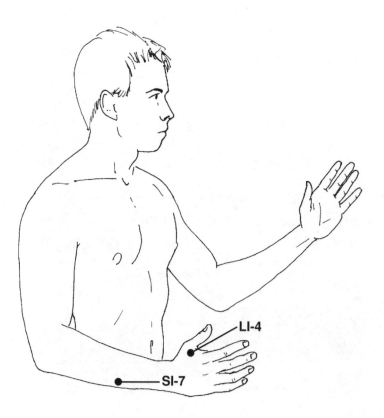

TECHNIQUE # 12

1. An attacker has grabbed your right wrist with his left hand.

2. Sweep your right hand up near your left shoulder to loosen his grip.

3. Reach underneath with your left hand and wrap your fingers around the thumb of his right hand, pressing on L-10 in the meat of the thumb.

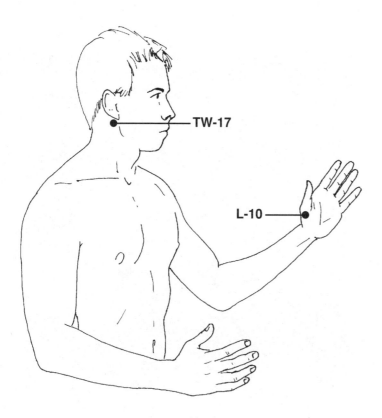

(Continued)

TECHNIQUE # 12 (Continued)

4-5. Draw his left hand toward your left hip, pulling the base of his thumb and turning his hand so the palm faces down (a basic "forearm turn"). This action exposes the attacker's head.

6. With your freed right hand, hammer down on TW-17 behind the opponent's jaw.

NOTE: Striking a person who has grabbed your wrist is justified only if you fear more serious assault.

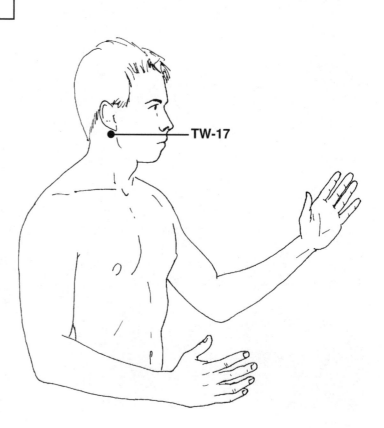

TECHNIQUE # 13

1. An attacker standing to your left, grabs your left wrist with his right hand (thumb down).

2. With your right hand, trap his left hand to your arm.

NOTE: This is a "cycle of destruction" technique working from a metal meridian (large intestine) to a wood meridian (gall bladder). See Advanced Pressure Point Fighting of RYUKYU KEMPO, pages 56-58.

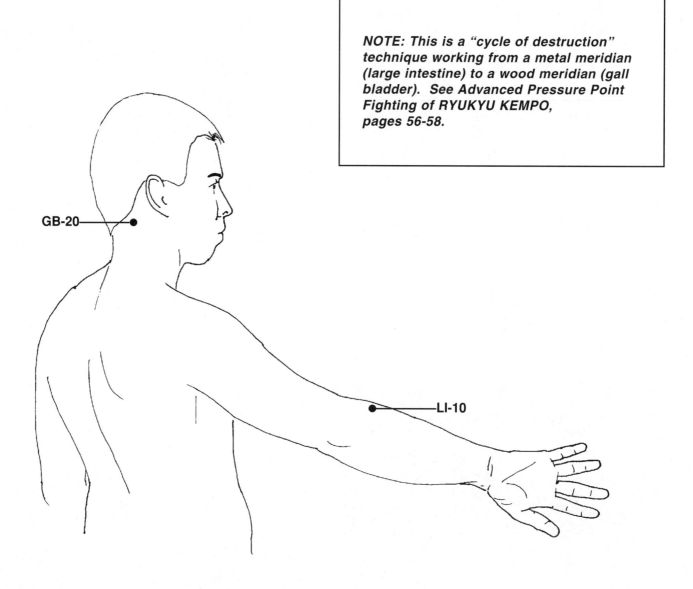

GB-20

LI-10

(Continued)

149

TECHNIQUE # 13 (Continued)

3-4. Bend your left elbow and roll it on top of the attacker's arm, and apply downward pressure on LI-10, and upward pressure on his captured hand. At this point you have applied the basic technique "wrist turn/press".

5. With your right hand jerk the attacker's right arm toward your right hip, and with your left fist strike GB-20 at the base of his skull.

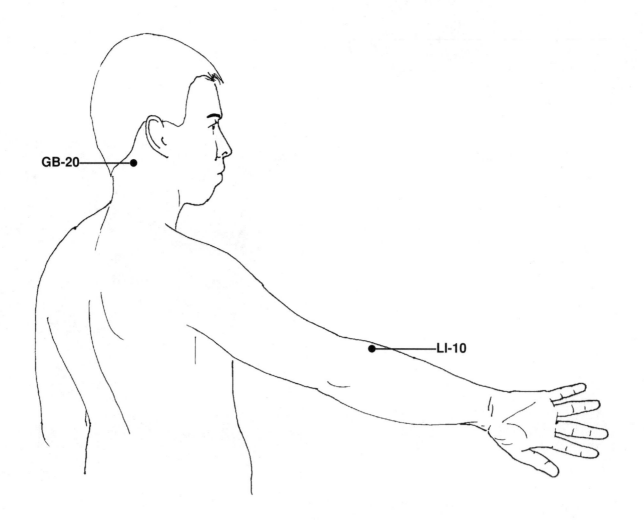

GB-20

LI-10

TECHNIQUE # 14

1. An attacker grabs your right arm near the elbow with his right hand.

2-4. Sweep your right forearm in a circular path up to shoulder level, trapping your attacker's hand in the bend of your elbow, and pressing your wrist against his forearm.

5-6. Pivot 90 degrees to your right turning your attacker and exposing his back to your counter-attack.

(Continued)

TECHNIQUE # 14 (Continued)

A-E The close-up photos show that the right arm movement is the basic karate technique commonly called "middle block." Clearly this is not a block. For more information on correct applications of this technique, see **KYUSHO-JITSU: The Dillman Method of Pressure Point Fighting,** pages 120-127.

[A-C] The bending and circling of the arm squeezes against the opponent's little finger.

[D] As you begin to turn, your forearm presses against the point SI-6 at his wrist.

[E] The opponent's body rotates, exposing his side and back to counter-attack. Punch to Li-13 or GB-25.

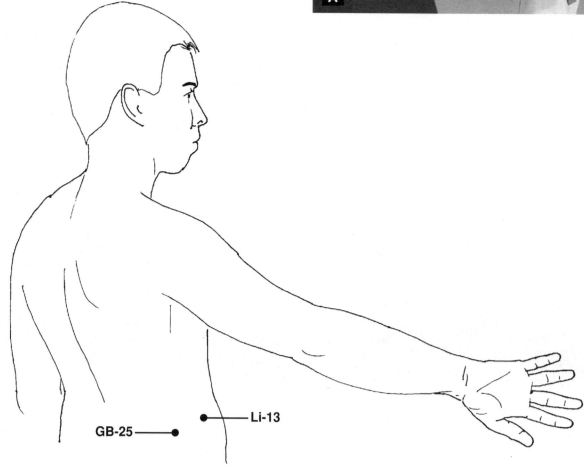

GB-25

Li-13

TECHNIQUE # 15

1. An assailant grabs your left arm near the elbow with his right hand.

2-3. Bring your left hand up on the inside of his arm, trapping his thumb in the crook of your elbow.

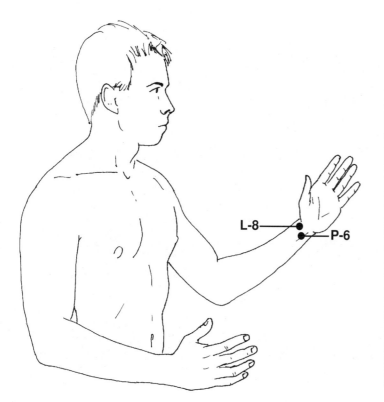

NOTE: The left forearm presses against the inside surface of the wrist stimulating, in particular, the lung and pericardium meridians (at points L-8 and P-6, respectively). Pericardium has the elemental value "fire", and lung has the value "metal". Metal is destroyed by fire (cycle of destruction), so the lung meridian is weakened by the stimulation of the pericardium channel, making the thumb completely vulnerable. The principle of attacking several points on the same meridian (in this case, pericardium) is discussed on pages 46-49 of *Advanced Pressure Point Fighting of RYUKYU KEMPO.*

Also, note the way in which the attacker's left arm swings away (crossed-extensor reflex), so that he is unable to defend in any fashion.

(Continued)

TECHNIQUE # 15 (Continued)

4-5. Sweep your left arm up to the level of your forehead, raising your opponent to his toes from the pressure on his thumb.

> **NOTE: This action is another of karate's so-called "blocks", usually called "upward", or "rising" block. For more on the correct usage of this technique, see KYUSHO-JITSU: The Dillman Method of Pressure Point Fighting, pages 140-149.**

6. Punch to the attacker's exposed chest, striking P-1.

CAUTION: Do not strike P-1 in practice.

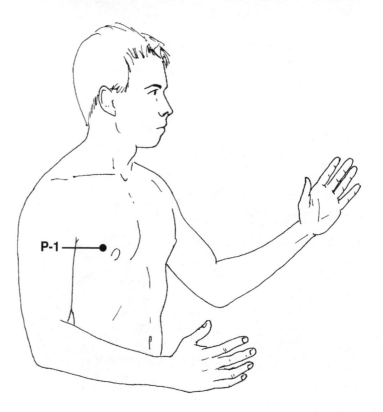

TECHNIQUE # 16

1. An assailant grabs your left arm near the elbow with his right hand.

2-3. Circle your left arm to the outside of your attacker's right arm.

> *NOTE: Moving from the triple warmer meridian to the gall bladder meridian follows the diurnal cycle of ki. See* **Advanced Pressure Point Fighting of RYUKYU KEMPO,** *pages 54-55.*

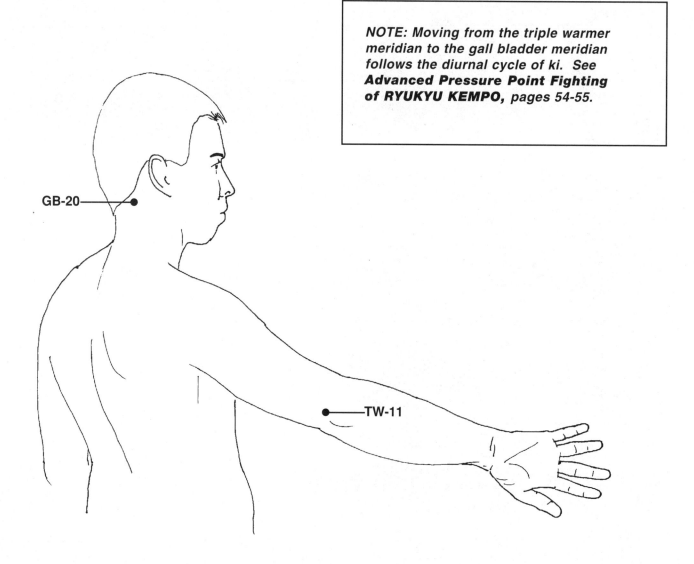

GB-20

TW-11

(Continued)

161

TECHNIQUE # 16 (Continued)

4-5. Bend your left arm and rub with your forearm across TW-11, to release his elbow and lock his arm against your chest.

> **NOTE: The application of this technique requires the use of muchimi, or "sticking", since you never grab onto your attacker's arm. Also, notice that his wrist is locked against your chest. This is the tuité principle "Creating a base".**

6. Punch the opponent on GB-20 at the base of the skull.

> **CAUTION: Do not actually punch GB-20 in practice.**

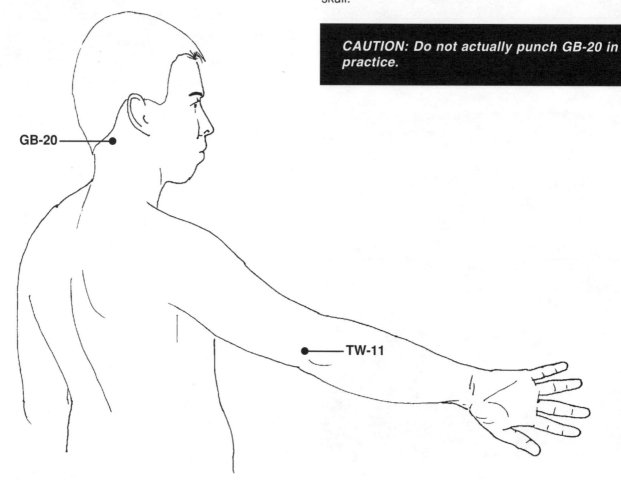

GB-20

TW-11

TECHNIQUE # 17

1-2. An attacker steps up and grabs you by the lapel with both hands.

3-5. Step forward with your left leg and punch with both hands using single knuckle fists to attack Li-13 at the lower edge of the rib cage.

CAUTION: Do not actually strike Li-13 in practice.

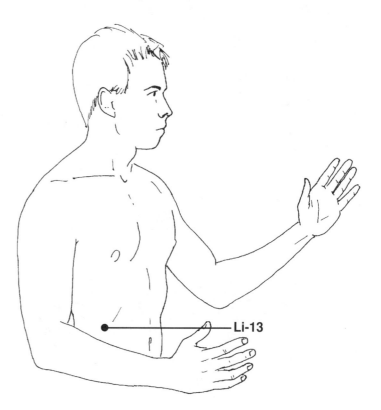

Li-13

(Continued)

TECHNIQUE # 17 (Continued)

6-7. Bring your left wrist over his right wrist and rotate his forearm downward while lifting his elbow with your right wrist.

8-9. Slide your left arm up underneath his elbow and put pressure on H-2, then turn to the right and apply a basic "shoulder lock".

10. Finish with a right punch to GB-20 at the base of the attacker's skull.

CAUTION: Do not actually strike GB-20 in practice.

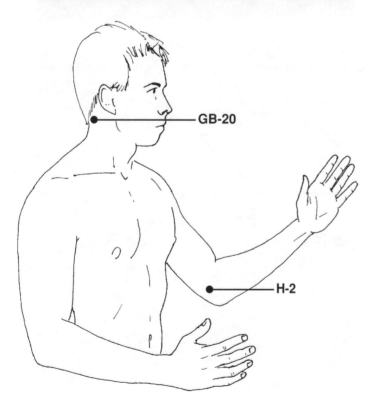

NOTE: This technique flows from point striking to joint manipulating to point striking. The attack to the body is a transitional move to secure the shoulder technique, which itself is a transitional move into the punch to the head. The principle of muchimi (sticking) is used in the application of the shoulder manipulation.

TECHNIQUE # 18

1. An assailant has grabbed your lapel with his right hand.

2-3. Using both your hands, trap and press the base of his palm flat against your body, leaning forward slightly so that his wrist bends.

4. Turn to your right using your body to press against the little finger of his clenched fist. Even though his hand is closed on your lapel, the angle of his wrist and the rotation against the little finger are the same as a palm turn.

NOTE: This technique is an example of a tuité progression, utilizing a "palm turn" to gain a "wrist turn/press". A tuité progression fulfills the requirement of creating a state of confusion in the opponent's body. As the "palm turn" is applied, his body turns to the side. Suddenly the pressure is released, and he begins to recover his posture. Then, just before he can regain himself, a new technique moves his body in a different direction.

CAUTION: Because this technique was photographed on a mat it was possible to execute the final "wrist turn/press" quickly (though still not at full speed). The "attacker" crashed down, landing forcefully on his elbow. Without the mat, his right arm would have been hurt. At full speed his left wrist would also have been hurt. This means that, by applying a single "wrist turn/press" it is possible to seriously injure both of your attacker's arms. For this reason, the utmost care must be used in practice.

(Continued)

TECHNIQUE # 18 (Continued)

5. Turn back slightly toward your left, releasing the pressure on his wrist, and peel his hand from your lapel (in shock from the palm turn, his hand will come away easily).

6. Rotate his hand clockwise (from your viewpoint) so that his thumb is down and his palm faces to your left.

7-9. Press upward with the thumb of your right hand on LI-4 and downward with your left hand on SI-6 (a small circle twist focused toward the opponent's center) to apply a basic "wrist turn/press" and drop the assailant to the ground.

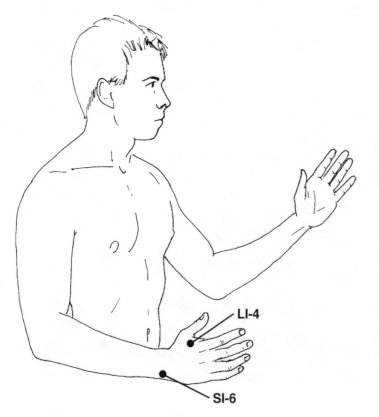

TECHNIQUE # 19

1. A particularly strong attacker grabs your lapel with his left hand.

2-3. You reach over with your left hand and grab his wrist on H-6, but are not able to loosen his grip.

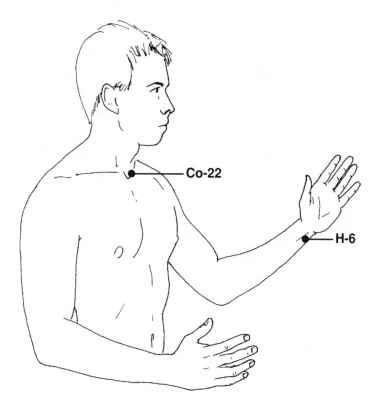

NOTE: The attack to Co-22 applies two of tuite's basic principles. The first principle is the use of pressure points. Attacking the conception meridian weakens all yin meridians, making them more vulnerable. Thus, a pressure point on the body is used to effect the flow of energy to the heart point at the wrist, which is used to weaken and release the grasp. Second, pressing on Co-22 causes pain and body movement, both of which work to create a state of confusion in the opponent's body and mind.

(Continued)

TECHNIQUE # 19 (Continued)

4. Without hesitation, plunge your extended index and middle fingers into Co-22 in the supra-sternal notch.

> *CAUTION: Be careful to press in and down to stimulate the pressure point, rather than in and up which can injure the esophagus.*

5. Re-grasp his wrist at H-6 and easily peel his hand off your lapel.

6. Apply the basic technique "wrist turn/press" to drop your assailant.

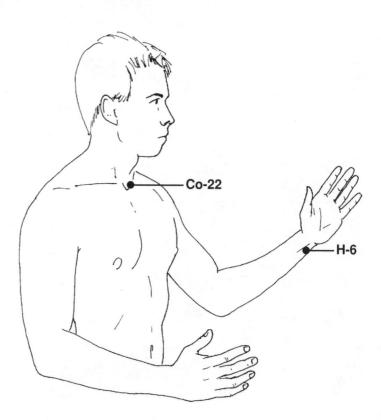

TECHNIQUE # 20

1. An assailant has grabbed your lapel with his right hand.

2-4. With your right hand strike down on L-5 at the crease of his left elbow, causing his body to spin.

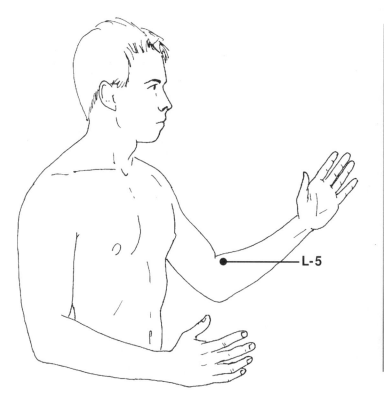

(Continued)

177

TECHNIQUE # 20 (Continued)

5. With your left hand seize the hair on the left-rear quadrant of his head.

6-8. In a sweeping movement, pull the attacker to the ground by his hair.

> **CAUTION: Always practice a technique involving the rotation of your opponent's neck and head with extreme care. Move slowly. Never jerk the head, or pull with force.**

TECHNIQUE # 21

1. An attacker has grabbed your lapel with both hands.

2-4. With your left hand reach over both his arms and strike LI-10 or LI-11 on the outside of his left forearm, near the elbow, to lower his left shoulder and turn his head to the right.

> *NOTE: In a single hand lapel grab a strike to L-5, a yin meridian point, works best. However, when the attacker grabs you with both hands it is as though the yang meridians short across your body. The yin meridian points become less responsive while the yang meridians become more responsive. This is why LI-10, or LI-11 are used, as the large intestine is a yang meridian. For more on yin and yang polarity refer to **Advanced Pressure Point Fighting of RYUKYU KEMPO,** pages 50-52.*

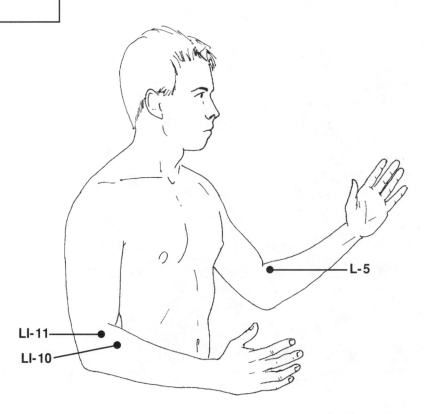

(Continued)

TECHNIQUE # 21 (Continued)

NOTE: For additional information on grabbing and controlling the head see *Advanced Pressure Point Fighting of RYUKYU KEMPO,* pages 110-113, and pages 266-271.

5. Reach up with your right hand and grab your attacker's hair, at the right rear quadrant of his head.

6-7. Draw his left elbow toward your left, while turning to your right and pulling his head in a sweeping movement to throw him to the ground.

The draw of the elbow to the left while you pull his head to the right creates two-way action.

8. Strike with your left hand to S-7 at the joint of the attacker's jaw with the knuckle of your thumb.

CAUTION: A strike downward on S-7 can dislocate the jaw. Always use care in practice.

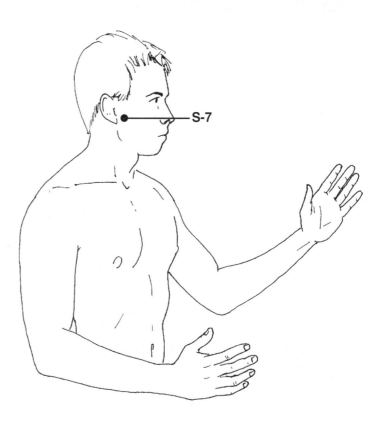

By locking his little finger, you take control of the encounter
and create the state of mental and physical confusion that will
allow you to complete your defense. The pain is excruciating!

TUITÉ SELF-DEFENSE AGAINST COMPLEX ATTACKS

In the previous chapter, the nature of the attacks was very simple. Actions of reaching and grabbing are relatively slow and easy to respond to. In this chapter the attacks (punches and grabs from behind) are more challenging, and require a greater level of skill.

TECHNIQUE # 22

1-3. As an assailant punches to your face with his right hand, deflect his attack to your right side by striking his arm at LI-7 with your left hand.

4. Brush your right arm along the outside of his arm with a heavy "sticky" feeling (muchimi).

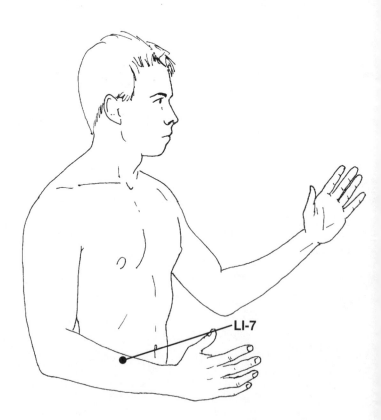

(Continued)

TECHNIQUE # 22 (Continued)

5-6. Maintaining contact between his arm and your right forearm, roll your hand over to grasp his wrist firmly at H-6 and L-8, and pull him forward.

7. Pull his captured hand to your right hip, turning it so his palm faces your body.

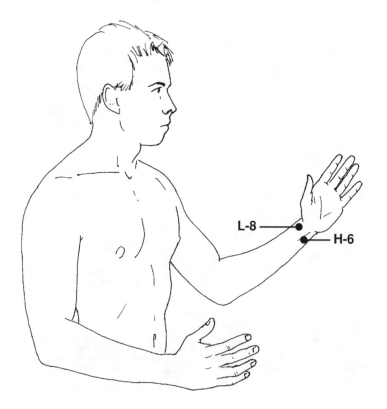

L-8

H-6

NOTE: This technique is called a "two-handed catch" or a "hand pass" and is discussed in Appendix B: How to Catch a Punch, in **KYUSHO-JITSU: The Dillman Method of Pressure Point Fighting.**

(Continued)

TECHNIQUE # 22 (Continued)

8-9. With the foreknuckles of your left fist, knead TW-11 at the triceps tendon to release his elbow and lock-out his arm.

10. Take a step forward and punch GB-20 at the base of the opponent's skull.

> **CAUTION: Do not actually punch GB-20 in practice.**

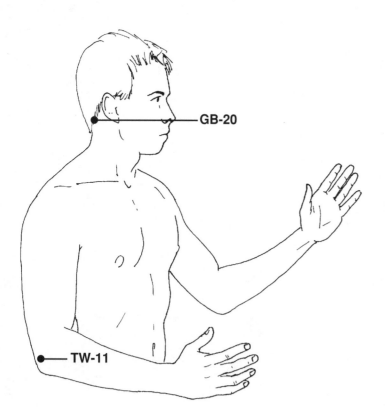

> **NOTE: Attacking the gall bladder meridian after attacking the triple warmer meridian follows the diurnal cycle of ki.**

TECHNIQUE # 23

1-2. As an assailant punches at you with his left hand, deflect his attack to your left by striking his arm at SI-7 with your right hand.

3. Maintain contact (muchimi) with your right arm on his forearm, and strike upward with your left fist at H-2 to bend his elbow.

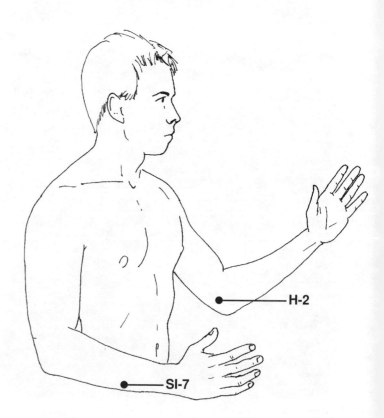

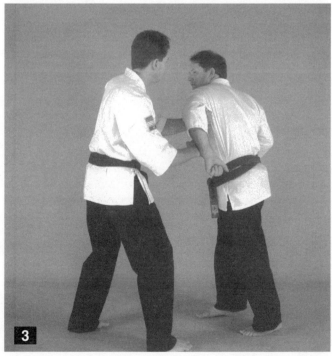

(Continued)

TECHNIQUE # 23 (Continued)

4. Press down on the attacker's forearm with your right wrist to rotate the arm at the shoulder (inward rotation) while stepping to his left side.

5-7. Thread your right arm under his forearm and over his upper arm, pressing on H-2 with your right fist to apply a basic shoulder lock. At the same time pivot on your right foot and turn toward your left, sweeping your left foot back to form a front stance.

8. With your left fist, punch to SI-16 on the side of the attacker's neck.

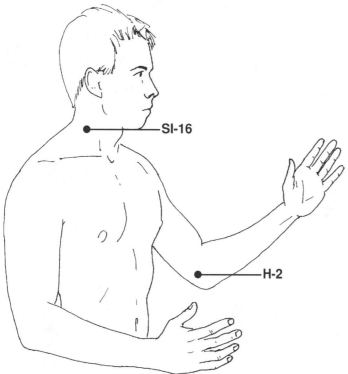

SI-16

H-2

NOTE: It is the hand motion (using muchimi) which applies the shoulder lock, but it is the footwork and body pivot that creates the pressure and controls the opponent. This is an example of the use of mechanical advantage in tuité.

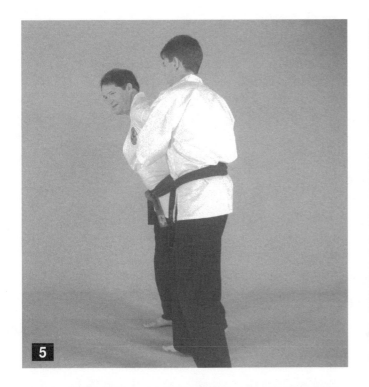

(Continued)

TECHNIQUE # 23 (Continued)

A-F Details of the hand movement to acquire the shoulder lock can be seen in close-up.

[A] It is striking H-2 with your left fist which bends the attacker's elbow. However, the right forearm also presses down near his wrist to create two-way action.

[B-C] The action of circling the attacker's left arm and threading your right arm through is a continuous motion.

[D-E] The key to a shoulder lock is controlling the opponent's elbow. This is done by maintaining pressure on H-2 and holding his elbow close to your body.

[F] SI-16 is attacked because of the relationship between the heart and small intestine meridians. The heart is yin and the small intestine is yang.

TECHNIQUE # 24

1. An assailant has grabbed you from behind, wrapping his arms around you, with his hands locked together, so that your arms are pinned against your body.

2-4. Attack the back of his right hand (the hand on the outside) with the foreknuckles of your right hand to loosen his grip. Aim particularly for TW-3 and M-UE-24.

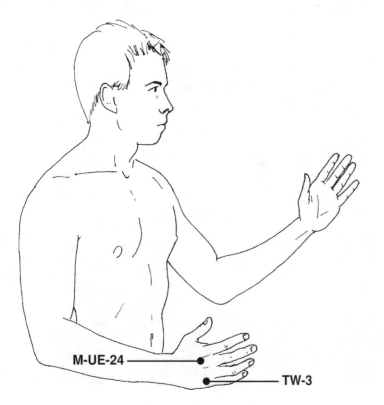

M-UE-24

TW-3

NOTE: *This technique can be done in two different ways. You may strike the back of his hand, in which case a single-point fist is the preferable hand formation (see appendix for information on this fist formation). Or, you may rub your knuckles laterally across the back of his hand, moving from M-UE-24 to TW-3 and back again.*

(Continued)

TECHNIQUE # 24 (Continued)

5. Grab his little finger (you may also grab his ring finger) and peel his right hand free.

6. Immediately create a base by using your left hand to control his palm, and lock his little finger.

7. Your left hand which created a base for the finger lock, now grabs all four fingers of the attacker's right hand. Be careful to squeeze the little finger behind the ring finger.

8. Step away from your attacker with your left foot and pivot to your right to face him. At the same time, lock onto his wrist at H-6 and L-8 with your right hand.

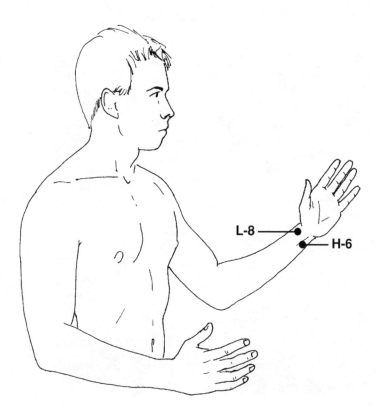

NOTE: By locking his little finger, (step 6) you take control of the encounter and create the state of mental and physical confusion that will allow you to complete your defense.

(Continued)

TECHNIQUE # 24 (Continued)

9-10. Perform a "palm turn" with particular emphasis on rotating his hand clockwise by pushing forward with your palm, while drawing his wrist close to your body (applying two-way action and working into your own natural mechanical advantage), to put the opponent on the ground in front of you.

NOTE: In photo 9 the speed with which the opponent falls is quite evident in the blurred motion of the attacker. The defender, however, appears perfectly still. This is an indication of one of the characteristics of tuité-waza: a small effort produces a great effect. Also, note the crossed-extensor reflex action as the attacker's left arm sweeps backwards.

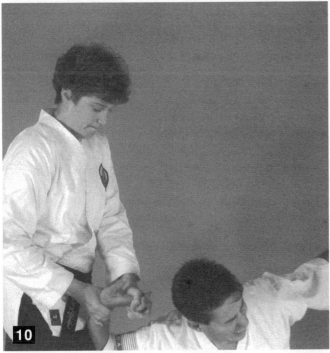

TECHNIQUE # 25

1. An assailant has grabbed you from behind, wrapping his arms around you, with his hands locked together, so that your arms are pinned against your body.

2. Strike the back of his left hand (the hand on the outside) successively with foreknuckles of both of your fists, aiming particularly for TW-3 and M-UE-24 until his grip loosens.

3. As he releases his hold, grab his left hand with your right hand and press down, while locking his elbow in the crook of your left elbow with a sharp jerking motion (Two-way action). At the same time, step to your right into a toe-out straddle stance.

4. Raise your right arm to clear the attacker's arms from your body and strike him in the groin with your left fist.

This is a good example of the use of tuité-waza as a transitional movement. The elbow is locked with a jerking action, but there is no attempt to maintain this hold. It serves the purpose of unbalancing the attacker and exposing him to the groin strike.

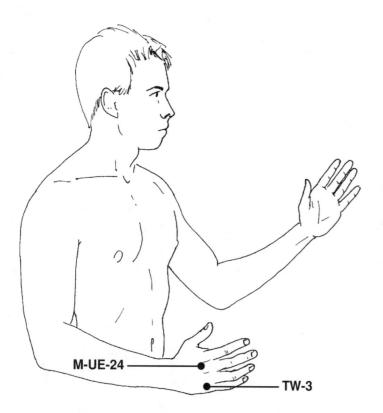

M-UE-24

TW-3

NOTE: In karate there are two types of straddle stances. One is positioned with the feet parallel to each other. The other has the feet angled outward at a 45 degree angle. This stance — called shiko-dachi — is used especially against attack from behind. This is because the outward angle of the legs draws vulnerable pressure points along the inner-thighs out of harm's way.

TECHNIQUE # 26

1. An attacker approaches from behind, reaching around to grab you.

2-3. Before he can complete his movement, sweep your hands up and apart to wedge your forearms outward against his grab.

NOTE: The skeletal mechanics are very important here because the opponent's action of wrapping and squeezing favors his movement, the strong muscular action called adduction. It is not possible for you, sweeping your arms outward (abduction), to resist his strong motion inward. Therefore, you must assume a body posture which is structurally stronger than his. To do this, your arms must find three 45 degree angles. First, your upper arm must be at a downward 45 degree angle to the vertical line of your body. Second, your elbow must be bent at 90 degrees so that your forearm is held at an upward 45 degree angle. Third, both arms must extend at 45 degrees to the centerline of your body.

With these angles in place, you must also be careful to connect with his arms on the back of the lower half of your forearm (in the area between your elbow and midway to the wrist). If you make contact nearer your wrist, he will be able to collapse your arms against your body.

(Continued)

TECHNIQUE # 26 (Continued)

4-5. Grab his fingers, particularly his little fingers, and bend his hands back.

6-7. Cross-step behind yourself with your left foot, while lifting his right arm over your head.

NOTE: Maintain painful control on both his hands by bending his fingers as if to point them at his shoulders (the fingers of his raised right hand aim down at his left shoulder, and the fingers of his left hand aim up toward his right shoulder).

(Continued)

TECHNIQUE # 26 (Continued)

8. Lower his right arm (continuing to point his fingers toward his shoulder) and sweep his left arm under his right arm, to cross it at H-2 above the elbow.

9-10. Push his left arm in a downward arc against his right arm, while pulling his right hand toward your right hip (two-way action).

This applies a compound technique consisting of a shoulder lock and a finger lock.

11. Releasing your hold, attack with a fingertip strike to SI-16 on the side of the neck.

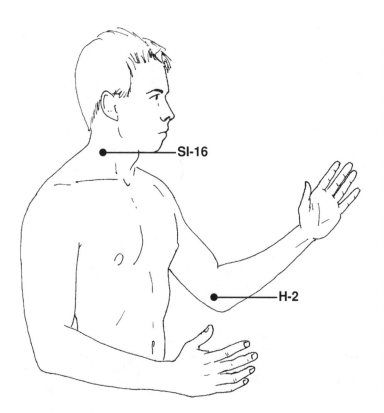

*NOTE: The lock attacks the heart meridian by bending the little finger and pressing on H-2. Heart is a yin meridian and its corresponding yang channel is small intestine, which is also stimulated by the pressure on the little finger, as well as the strike to the neck. Refer to **Advanced Pressure Point Fighting of RYUKYU KEMPO,** pages 50-52.*

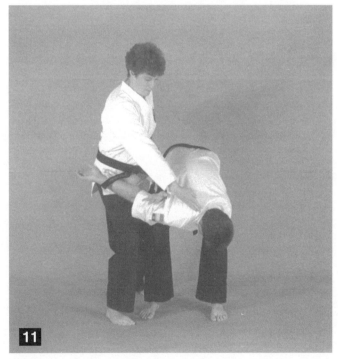

TECHNIQUE # 27

1. An attacker grabs your right shoulder from behind with his right hand (though you do not know it is his right hand).

2-3. Raise your right arm as if performing a so-called "upward block".

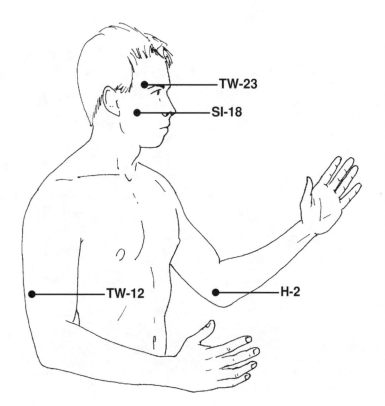

TW-23

SI-18

TW-12

H-2

The following three examples use the same initial response, even though the attack varies in each case. This is a feature of good technique because it reduces reaction time by eliminating the problem of having to choose the right defensive response.

(Continued)

TECHNIQUE # 27 (Continued)

4-5. Stepping behind with your right foot, and pivoting on your left, turn to face your opponent. At the same time, bring your raised right arm over his forearm.

6. Draw your right elbow to your hip, stripping the attacker's hand from your shoulder and trapping his arm in your armpit.

7. With your left hand, strike his upper arm, to jar his elbow and shoulder.

Strike either H-2 (as shown) or TW-12, depending on how much his arm turns as it is being trapped.

8. With your right hand strike your attacker's face.

NOTE: Punching the face is an invitation to a broken hand. However, pressure point strikes do not require full power, so they can be delivered to the head without fear of injury. If in step # 7, you attacked H-2, then attack below the cheek-bone at SI-18 with the punch (as shown). If your attack to his arm was aimed at TW-12, then attack the temple at TW-23.

TECHNIQUE # 28

1. An attacker grabs your right shoulder from behind with his left hand (though you do not know it is his left hand).

2. Raise your right arm as if performing a so-called "upward block".

3-4. Pivot to your right, bringing your right arm over the attacker's arm and down, to strip his hand from your shoulder and trap his arm against your side.

5. With your left palm, strike the corner of the jaw upward at SI-17 on the left side of the attacker's face.

NOTE: As you turn, your raised right arm sweeps across at head level, providing protection against a punch to the head.

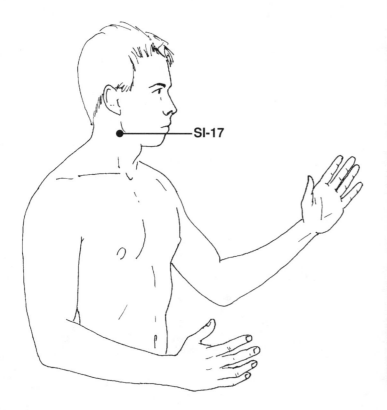

SI-17

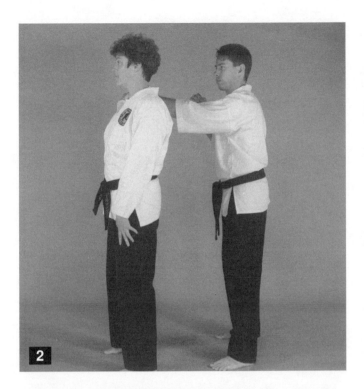

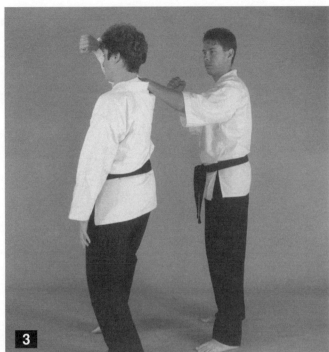

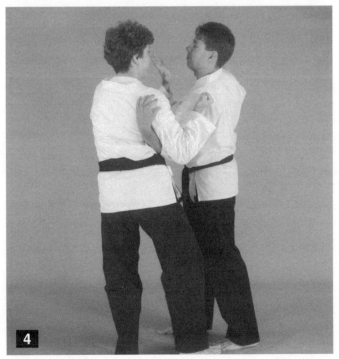

TECHNIQUE # 29

1. An attacker grabs your shoulders from behind with both hands.

2-4. Step back with your right foot and turn, sweeping your arm up and over his arms.

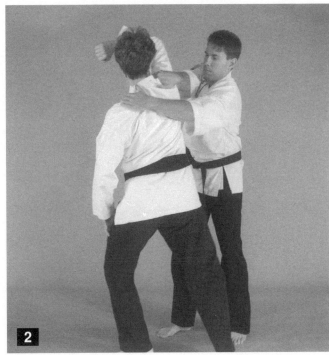

(Continued)

TECHNIQUE # 29 (Continued)

5. Draw your right elbow to your hip, stripping the attacker's hands from your shoulders and trapping them against your side.

6. With your left hand, punch strongly to his ribs, striking GB-24/Li-14 (these two points are close together so that your fist connects with both at the same time).

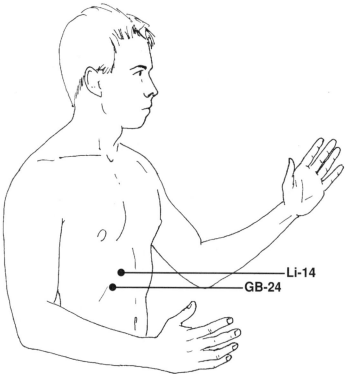

Li-14
GB-24

TECHNIQUE # 30

1. An assailant reaches around to grab you from behind.

2-4. Bring your left arm up diagonally, trapping his left arm against your upper chest.

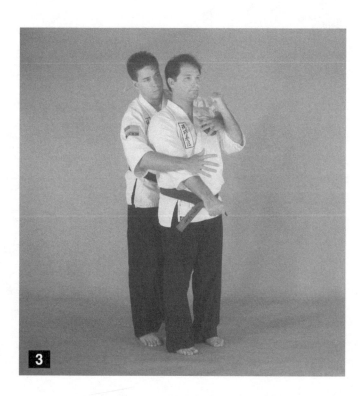

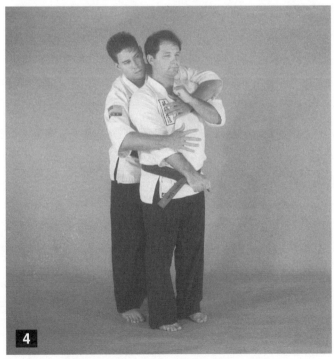

(Continued)

223

TECHNIQUE # 30 (Continued)

5-6. Pivot to your right, then step back with your right foot, ducking under his captured left arm. During this motion, strike with your elbow to the opponent's groin.

7. Take one step diagonally back with your left foot, stretching his left arm, his hand bent back against your chest.

(Continued)

225

TECHNIQUE # 30 (Continued)

8. Knead TW-11 just above the attacker's elbow, driving him down against the bend of his trapped fingers (this is a compound technique, elbow lock and finger lock).

CAUTION: Kneading TW-11 can cause the attacker's shoulder to release suddenly and uncontrollably. The rapid drop of his body could dislocate his trapped fingers. Use the utmost care in practice.

9. Step forward and punch the opponent in the base of the skull at GB-20.

NOTE: The groin is associated with the kidney meridian, so attacking first the groin, then the triple warmer works from a water element to a fire element. This follows the cycle of destruction. Attacking the triple warmer then the gall bladder follows the diurnal cycle.

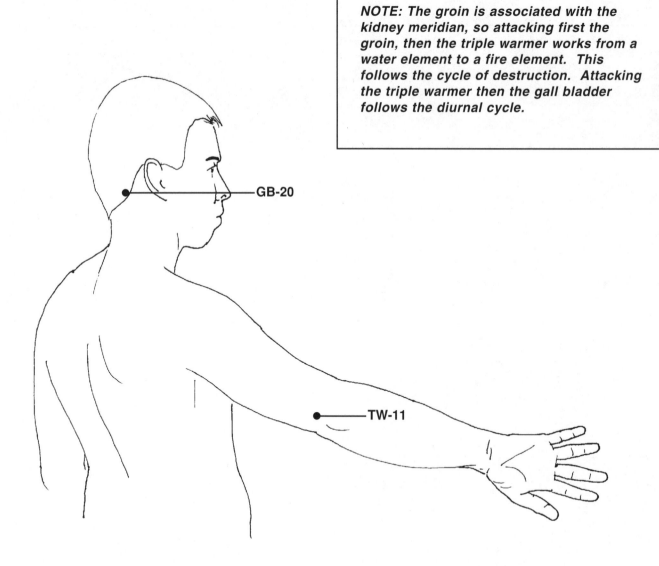

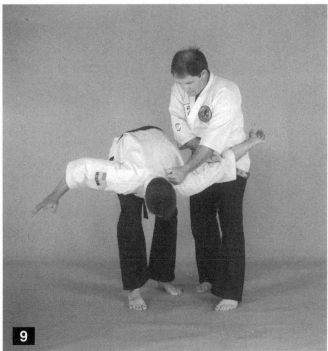

TECHNIQUE # 31

1-2. An attacker reaches to grab you from behind, his left arm encircling your left arm, and his right arm passing under your upraised arm.

3. Drop your right arm in a hooking motion, trapping his right arm against your body.

4-5. Reaching across with your left hand (thumb down), grab the fingers of the attacker's right hand and apply a basic "palm turn".

(Continued)

TECHNIQUE # 31 (Continued)

6-8. Pivoting on your right foot, step in a circular motion 225 degrees to your right.

> **CAUTION:** *With his arm trapped against your body and his hand locked in a palm turn, a rapid 225 degree turn can injure his wrist. Use the utmost care in practice, and appropriate restraint in self-defense.*

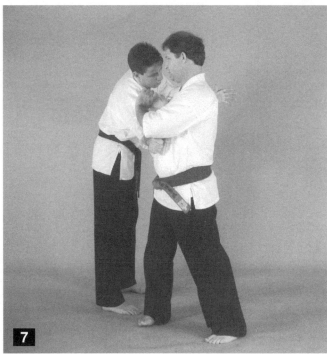

(Continued)

TECHNIQUE # 31 (Continued)

9. Sweep your right forearm down, striking the attacker at the side of the biceps on LI-13, driving him to his knees.

10-12. With your right fist, strike the attacker at the base of the skull on GB-20.

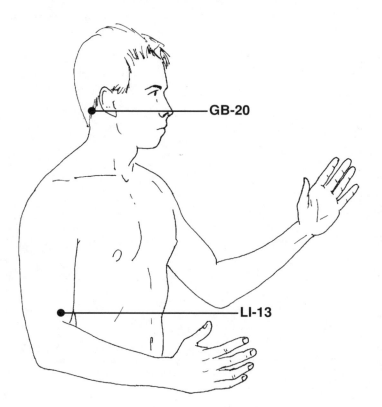

GB-20

LI-13

NOTE: The striking motion is the movement mistakenly called "downward block" in karate. For more information on the correct applications of this technique see **KYUSHO-JITSU: The Dillman Method of Pressure Point Fighting,** pages 112-119, 194-201, 266-267.

The pressure point attack begins on the heart meridian in the little finger, then proceeds to the large intestine meridian on the upper arm and finishes with the gall bladder meridian on the head. This sequence follows the cycle of destruction; fire, metal, wood.

Barbara Converse (weighs less than 100 lbs.) uses pressure points to knock out Mark Krar during a Chicago area demonstration by the team from Bob "Pitt Bull" Golden's school.

ADVANCED CONCEPTS IN TUITÉ

Up to this point, the techniques described have emphasized hand work. The function of the legs has been turning and pivoting the body to obtain better angles against the joints; however, the legs can be used to enhance the effectiveness of a technique.

TECHNIQUE # 32

1. An assailant is jabbing his right index finger into your face.

2. Bring your left hand up and trap his wrist.

3-4. Immediately grasp his extended finger with your right hand, digging with a fingertip into either M-UE-22 or M-UE-24 to release the knuckle joint. At the same time, lock the fingers of your left hand onto the opponent's pressure point L-8, as you step forward with your left foot into a cat stance.

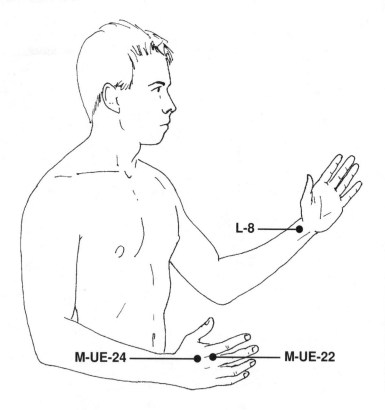

L-8

M-UE-24 — *M-UE-22*

NOTE: L-8 is used because the lung meridian is related to the large intestine meridian which travels up the index finger.
In the case of a large opponent, you may step back into the cat stance, using body movement to pull his finger away from his strength and into yours (mechanical advantage). This also creates confusion in his body by over-extending his balance.

(Continued)

TECHNIQUE # 32 (Continued)

5. With a sharp torque of the right hand, apply two-way action against his index finger, while drawing his wrist toward your body with your left hand.

6. Lock his wrist against your left thigh (create a base), and apply pressure against the base of his index finger toward your leg.

NOTE: At this point you can easily inflict injury to his finger, but only if absolutely necessary to insure your safe escape.

In martial arts training, a great deal of attention is devoted to perfecting stances. This technique, reveals the reason for such training: the cat stance is ideally suited to this application.

TECHNIQUE # 33

1. An assailant has grabbed your right wrist with his right hand.

2. Step forward with your left leg, lightly treading on the attacker's right foot to pin it to the floor, and reach your left arm under his right.

In step 2, it is possible to strike Li-13, with your left hand as part of the stepping motion — for instant distraction.

3. Turn 180 degrees to your right into a cat stance, and draw his right arm across your center, so that his grip is loosened.

NOTE: As you draw his right arm around, apply slight counter-pressure against his elbow with your left arm to briefly apply a front shoulder lock.

(Continued)

TECHNIQUE # 33 (Continued)

4. With your left hand, grab the attacker's little and ring fingers, and peel his right hand from your wrist.

5-6. With your right hand guide his elbow back into the crook of your left arm as you apply a chicken wing (supination of the forearm with dorsiflexion of the wrist).

NOTE: At this point your opponent is helpless because pinning his foot does not allow him any means to escape the pressure of the chicken wing. You may simply apply variable pressure on his hand until he submits.

TECHNIQUE # 34

1. An attacker reaches for you with his right hand.

2-3. Intercept it with your left hand (thumb down) pressing your palm against his fingers. At the same time, grasp his wrist with your right hand, squeezing your fingertips into H-6 on his wrist and digging your thumb into LI-4 in the web of his thumb.

4. Using your right hand, pull his wrist toward your body, twisting his fingers with your left hand (complex torque), as you apply a basic "palm turn." At the same, tread lightly on the attacker's right foot at GB-41 with your left heel.

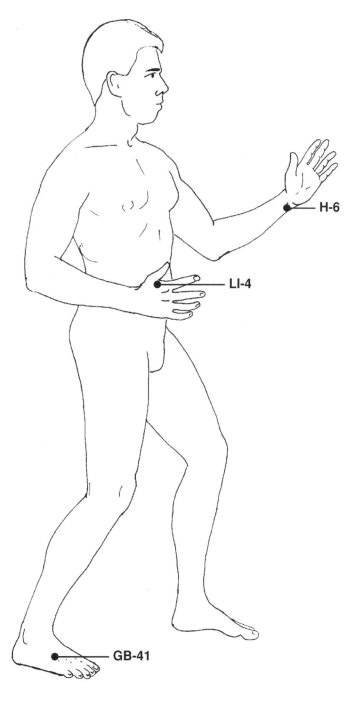

(Continued)

TECHNIQUE # 34 (Continued)

5. Grind your heel into GB-41 while twisting his captured hand and drawing it to your right hip.

6. With your left hand, chop the attacker's neck at LI-18.

7. Finish with a right punch to GB-20.

CAUTION: Do not strike GB-20 in practice.

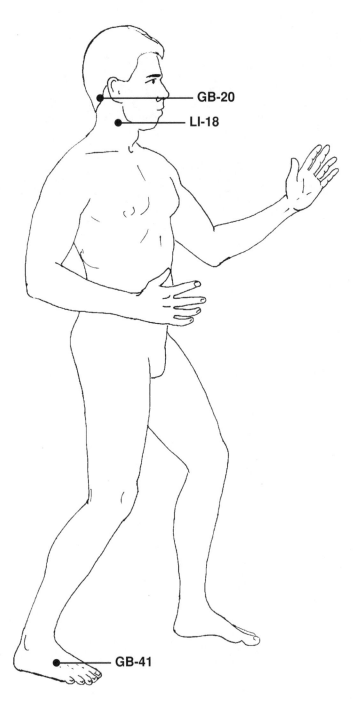

GB-20

LI-18

GB-41

NOTE: These two examples illustrate how stepping on an attacker's foot is a simple and effective self-defense method. A soft step can be enough to pin an attacker to the ground and disrupt his balance. Grinding the heel into GB-41 can cause intense pain. Either way, if a joint technique is executed on the arm while the foot is pinned, it is possible to injure the ankle.

TECHNIQUE # 35

This technique is a variation on technique # 27.

1. As an attacker reaches around to grab you from behind, sweep your hands up in a circular motion and wedge your forearms outward against his arms.

2. Grab his fingers, particularly his little fingers, and bend his hands back.

3-4. Sweep his right hand up over your head, and his left hand across his body. At the same time, turn to your left and sweep your left leg back, kicking his right foot out from under him.

> **NOTE: This creates two-way action in the opponent's body, his upper body moving one direction, his lower body moving the other.**

(Continued)

TECHNIQUE # 35 (Continued)

5. Lock his left arm against his right, just above the elbow at H-2.

6. Releasing your hold, shoot a finger-tip strike to SI-16 on the side of the neck.

> **NOTE: In step 5, you have applied a compound technique consisting of an elbow lock and a palm turn.**

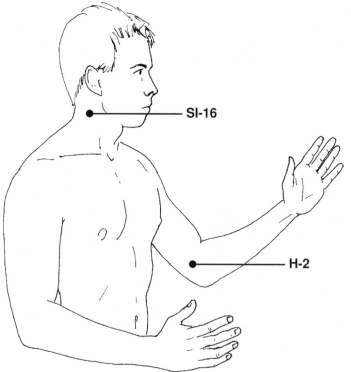

TECHNIQUE # 36

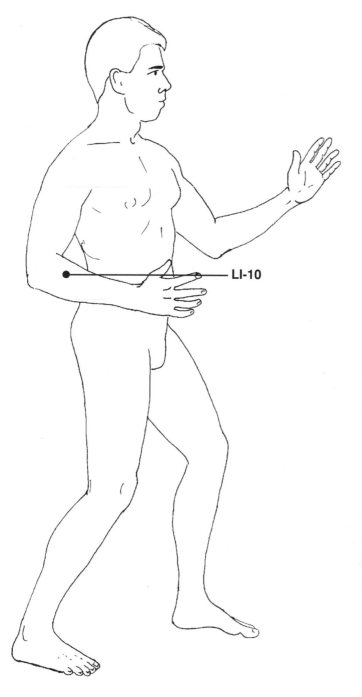

LI-10

NOTE: Tuité-waza can be applied with the legs as well as the hands, as the following illustrates.

1. An attacker grabs your lapel with his right hand.

2-3. With your left hand strike his arm near the elbow at LI-10.

4. Step forward with your right foot, placing it inside his right foot.

3

(Continued)

TECHNIQUE # 36 (Continued)

5. Bend your right knee and place it on the outside of the attacker's right knee at point N-LE-7.

6. Shift your weight forward and turn your knee outward, bending the attacker's leg inward at an unnatural angle.

7. Step diagonally forward with your left foot, and crouch down onto your opponent's right knee.

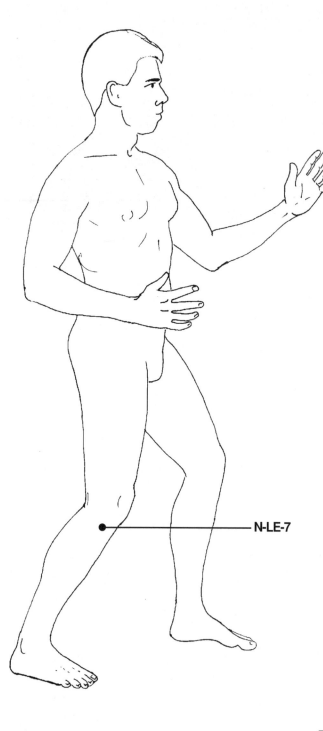

N-LE-7

NOTE: To prevent injuring your own joints, make sure to pivot on the balls of your feet, so they point in the same direction as your knees.

(Continued)

TECHNIQUE # 36 (Continued)

NOTE: The kneeling stance is common in martial arts. It is not intended for ducking under an attack (a common misconception). It is particularly suited to this application.

A-E In close-up, the details of this leg lock are apparent.

[A,B] The placement of your foot against the inside of the attacker's foot is very deliberate and done by feel as is the placement of the knee on the outside of his knee.

[C,D] The outward turning action of your knee and the shifting of your weight forward are small movements, but they have a significant effect on the opponent's body.

[E] In actual application, kneel down on the attacker's leg, driving it into the floor. The pain is excruciating, so use care in practice.

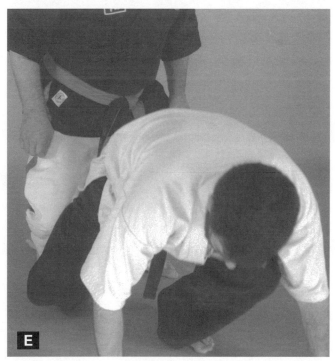

(Continued)

TECHNIQUE # 36 (Continued)

F-H A slight variation of this technique reveals something of its foolproof nature.

[F] After placing your foot to the inside and your knee to the outside of your opponent's leg, lean your weight forward, straightening his leg and shifting his weight back.

[G,H] With him off-balance, turn your knee and hips, and kneel down on his leg. In this case the original order of movements (turning your knee out, shifting your weight) has been reversed; yet, the technique still works.

TECHNIQUE # 37

1. An assailant has grabbed your lapel with his right hand, intending to punch with his left.

2. As the attacker punches to your head, strike his wrist at P-6 with your right hand, and step forward with your right foot, hooking it behind his lead leg.

NOTE: The chop to the wrist stops the attack from reaching your head, while setting up the succeeding movements.

3-4. Grab his wrist with your right hand. Press your left knee against his right leg just below and outside the knee-cap on N-LE-7 trapping his leg. Punch to TW-17 below his right ear with your left fist.

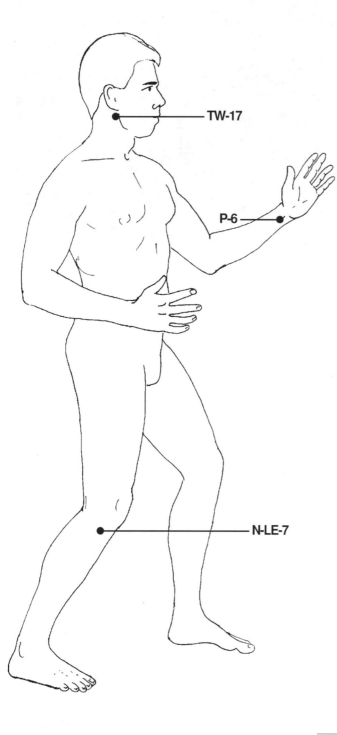

TW-17

P-6

N-LE-7

(Continued)

TECHNIQUE # 37 (Continued)

A-B In close-up the details of this leg trap are evident.

[A] Hook your right foot behind his right foot, by turning your right heel inward.

[B] Press your left knee forward through the crook of your right knee to apply pressure against the trapped leg.

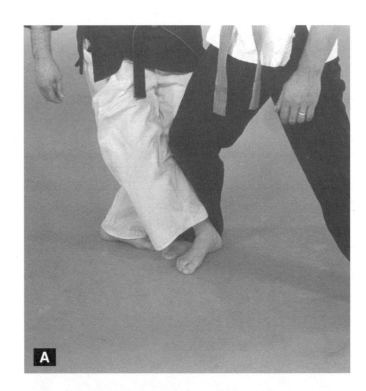

NOTE: This technique utilizes a basic cross-legged stance.

TECHNIQUE # 38

This technique, a favorite of many Okinawan teachers, requires much training and practice to successfully capture the leg.

1. An assailant attacks with a kick to your groin.

2. Catch the kick between your legs by squeezing the inner-thigh muscles tightly. (This takes a lot of practice.)

3. Cross your left foot over your right, trapping his leg.

4. Shift your weight onto your left foot as you attack his neck and jaw with a right "cupped hand" strike (hitting with the knuckle of your thumb at S-5 and the base of your little finger at S-9) while pressing your fingertips behind the knot of his belt at Co-3.

NOTE: The trapping action stimulates the three yin meridians (liver, spleen and kidney) on the inside of the leg and the gall bladder meridian on the outside. Point Co-3 is the "intersection point" of the three yin meridians on the conception channel which is why it is attacked subsequent to the leg trap. Attacking the stomach meridian works a cycle of destruction from the gall bladder meridian (wood to earth).

See the appendix for information on the "cupped hand" formation.

TECHNIQUE # 39

1-3. An assailant kicks to your groin with his right leg.

4. Bring your left knee in toward your centerline, and squeeze the tops of your thighs together.

NOTE: This is a more advanced leg-catch than the preceding example.

NOTE: This is the part of the technique that stops the kick, and must be done strongly. The feeling of squeezing the legs is the same as the cross-over catch described in the previous technique, but the feet do not cross.

(Continued)

TECHNIQUE # 39 (Continued)

5. Lift your right foot and hook it around your right knee, keeping pressure on the opponent's captured foot.

This is a basic crane stance.

6-8. Twist your body sharply to the right, twisting the assailant's leg along with you, and throwing him to the ground.

NOTE: The leg technique may be combined with hand techniques, with great effect [A].

TECHNIQUE # 40

> **NOTE: Tuité techniques are especially useful against multiple attackers, because they allow you to control the direction of your opponent's fall.**

1. Faced with two assailants, position yourself in front of the attacker on your left (rather than standing within reach of both).

2. As the closer attacker reaches out with his right hand, intercept it with your left palm (thumb down).

3. Reach over his wrist with your right hand, locking on H-6 and L-8.

4. Twist back against his little finger and pull his wrist slightly toward your body to apply a palm turn.

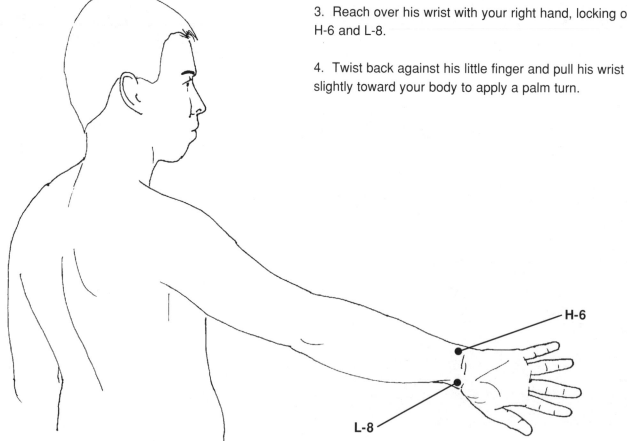

H-6

L-8

(Continued)

TECHNIQUE # 40 (Continued)

5-6. As the attacker's body reacts to the technique, drive his locked hand to his right shoulder, and turn sharply to your right, sending him into his partner, knocking them both down.

TECHNIQUE # 41

1. You are confronted by two assailants. The one to your right, throws a left punch at your head.

2. Using a one-handed catch, deflect and grab his left wrist at L-8 and H-6, pulling his arm to your left so it acts as a barrier between you and the second attacker.

> *NOTE: Refer to pages 264-267 of* ***KYUSHO-JITSU: The Dillman Method of Pressure Point Fighting****, for a description of the one-handed catch.*

3. Strike the triceps of your attacker's arm at TW-12, locking his arm and sending him into his partner.

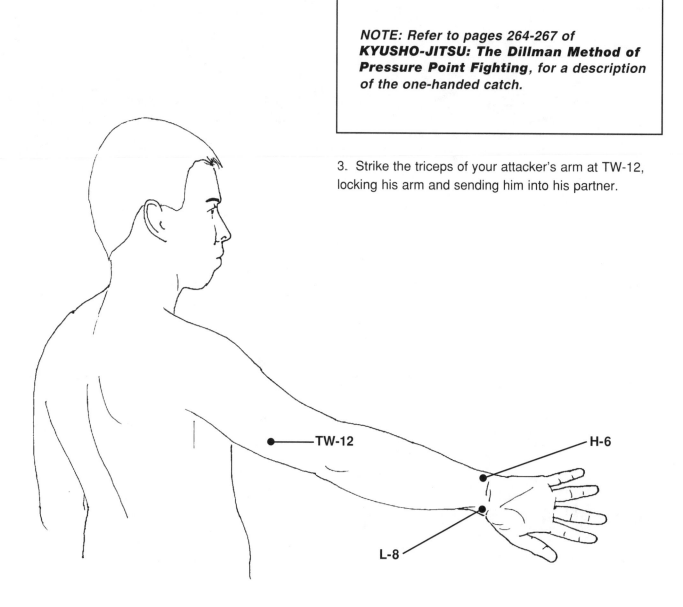

(Continued)

TECHNIQUE # 41 (Continued)

4-5. With your right palm, strike the second assailant on the jaw at S-5.

6. Immediately grab the second man's head and twist it sharply to your right, using a basic head turn to throw him toward the first attacker.

CAUTION: Use restraint in practice and do not strike S-5.

NOTE: When you strike the second man on S-5, his body will react by moving to your left. When you apply the head turn you are reversing his direction. This sudden reversal can result in serious injury to his neck. However, multiple attackers represent a threat to your life and may necessitate such a response.

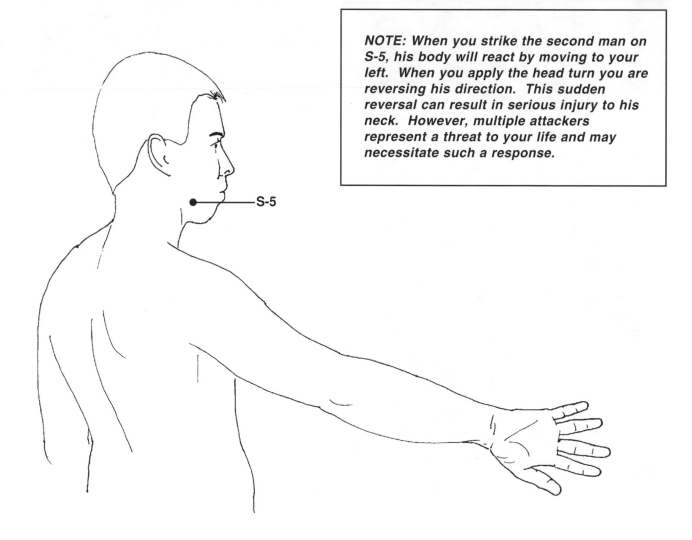

S-5

Gearge Dillman uses the pressure points and actions of tuité, to drop tw[o] opponents at the same time.

TUITÉ AS BUNKAI

The ancient masters of Ryukyu kempo passed on their fighting techniques in the form of fixed patterns of movements called kata. Kata consist of a series of techniques, performed in an established sequence. The order in which the movements are placed is somewhat arbitrary. A given self-defense sequence might involve only two postures while the kata itself may have twenty to sixty postures. The small groups of movements which make up a self-defense sequence are simply strung together like pearls to form the kata.

Historical evidence suggests that the earliest form of a kata was not the complete pattern that we know today, but rather a curriculum consisting of combative sequences. The students would learn a sequence, practice its application with a partner, then move on to the next sequence. In many cases, it is likely that the teacher did not actually develop the kata as such. Rather, it was the students who, in honor of their master, organized the techniques into a complete form.

Originally, the physical movements and the applications were taught together. But, later on it became the custom to teach the movements first and to teach the applications sometime after. This allowed a student's training to progress even while his or her character was being evaluated. In this way, the instructor had time to determine if the student was worthy to learn the secrets of the style.

All too often, however, students left their teachers after learning the physical movements, but before being introduced to their secret applications. In this way the outward form of the kata movements survived, but the true meanings were lost. However, because the kata possess an aesthetically pleasing quality, and were valued as a legacy of the old masters, they were prized even in their incomplete form.

The end of this process came with the introduction of karate-do. In the context of an art committed to discipline and control, the aesthetics and fixed nature of unexplained kata well suited the needs of the school-children's art. The question of meaning and interpretation was no longer significant.

By applying the concepts of kyusho-jitsu and tuité-jitsu to kata interpretation, it is possible to reclaim the original purpose of the forms. Genuine combative applications emerge which can be practiced with a partner and envisioned during solo training. In this chapter, we present short sequences from different kata. First we describe the movements themselves as they are performed in solo practice. Then we describe their use in practical self-defense, paying careful attention to the principles at work. Attention to principles will, we hope, equip readers to find tuité applications in any kata.

It is not necessary for the reader to study the kata which we include, or even any kata at all. These movements can simply be practiced with a partner just like any of the other techniques we have presented so far. (In fact, many of the techniques in the previous chapters are taken directly from various kata. Knowledgeable readers may be able to identify the sources of the movements.) It is our experience that the best practitioners of kyusho-jitsu and tuité-jitsu are those who study and practice kata the most diligently.

In describing kata movements, a language problem arises. Most techniques are known by common names, such as "middle block." But these often mistranslate the original Okinawan titles. In particular, the term "block" is a completely erroneous rendering of the Okinawan word "uke". Uke actually means "to receive", and thus "chudan uke" would mean "middle (level) receiving." A better English equivalent would be "middle response."

However, the term "response" is completely neutral, and so does nothing to mentally and emotionally equip a martial artist for combat. In contrast, a pro-active word, such as "counter", helps to program the mind to seize the initiative at an attacker's slightest aggression. For this reason, the word "uke" will be rendered "counter"; thus chudan uke, becomes "middle counter."

(Continued)

TECHNIQUE # 42
From Taikyoku Shodan

The Taikyoku kata were developed by Gichin Funakoshi as simple forms to teach beginners. However, the techniques from these kata are actually sophisticated self-defense maneuvers.

1. Stand upright with your fists extended in front.

2. Look to your left, drawing your right fist toward the left, and raising your left fist up toward your right ear.

3. With your left foot, step to the left side into a front stance, and perform a downward counter (gedan barrai uke) by sweeping your left arm down over your left foot, while drawing your right hand to your hip.

(Continued)

283

TECHNIQUE # 42 (Continued)
From Taikyoku Shodan

BUNKAI

1. An assailant grabs your right wrist with his left hand.

2-3. By stepping with your right foot, then sliding your left up to it, move to your attacker's side. At the same time, raise your right hand, rolling his arm over, and trapping it against your body with pressure on P-6.

> **NOTE: In the kata the first action is to look to the left side. This does not mean that an attack is coming from the left. Rather, it means that you must position yourself so that you are sideways to your opponent. The kata tells you how you are to be oriented in relation to your attacker, but does not dictate a particular means of achieving that orientation.**

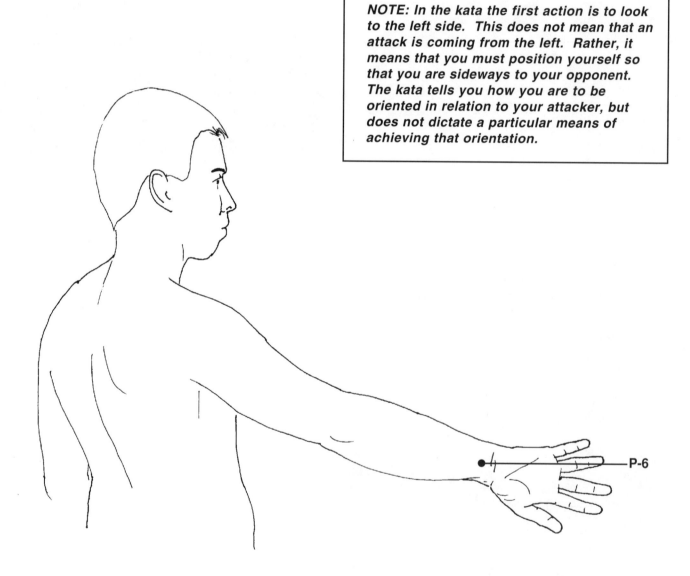

(Continued)

285

TECHNIQUE # 42 (Continued)
From Taikyoku Shodan

BUNKAI

4-5. Crash downward with your left elbow, striking the opponent's triceps at TW-12.

The left hand can also strike as it is being raised, so no motion is wasted. Such an attack is made in anticipation of the blow to TW-12, and so is aimed at points on the pericardium (yin/yang & diurnal cycle) or kidney (cycle of destruction) meridians. Because the heart meridian and the triple warmer meridian both have the elemental value fire, heart points may also be attacked prior to the TW-12 strike.

6-7. Stepping toward the attacker, smash your left fist down onto his back, hitting over his left kidney at GB-25.

> **NOTE: The progression of triple warmer to gall bladder follows the diurnal cycle.**

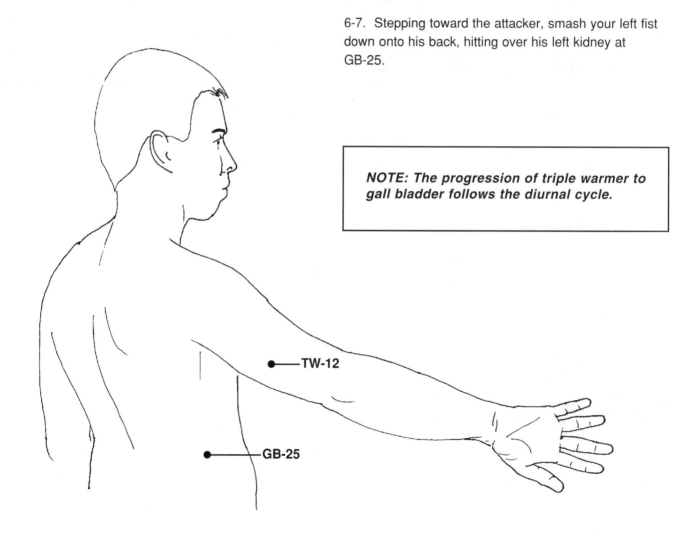

TW-12

GB-25

TECHNIQUE # 43
From Pinan Yondan

The Pinan kata were developed by Anko Itosu in 1907 and became part of his school-children's karate-do curriculum. This fact has led some to conclude that the Pinan forms do not contain any fighting secrets. Nothing could be further from the truth. The Pinan kata were not more appropriate for children because they were less deadly than other kata, but because they were shorter. The movements of these kata are based on older forms. One common theory is that Itosu based his Pinan forms on a kata called Kushanku-dai. Another explanation is that Itosu was re-working a lengthy Chinese form called Chiang Nan, restructuring it into five manageable units.

Despite the fact that the movements of the Pinan forms are every bit as deadly as those of any other traditional kata, it was a simple matter to keep children from learning these fighting secrets. They were simply misled with pointless "block, punch" explanations.

1-2. From a left front stance, shoot both open hands straight forward.

3. Bring your right knee up sharply and smash downward with your hands.

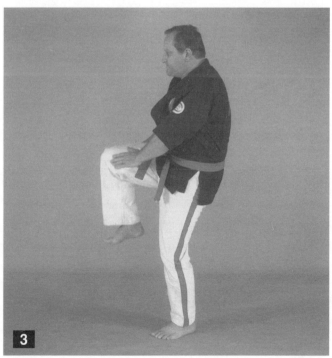

(Continued)

TECHNIQUE # 43 (Continued)

From Pinan Yondan

4-6. Pivoting 180 degrees to your left, perform a left knife-hand counter (shuto uke).

(Continued)

TECHNIQUE # 43 (Continued)
From Pinan Yondan

BUNKAI

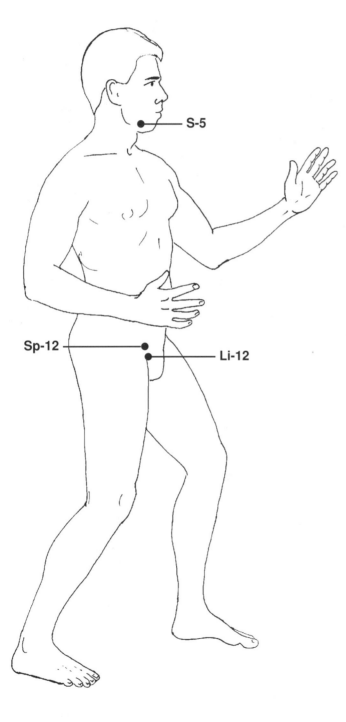

1. An assailant has grabbed your lapels.

2-4. Strike upward, hitting the opponent at S-5 on both sides of his jaw.

> **CAUTION: Never strike both S-5 points in practice!**

5. Strike with your knee into the crease of the leg, at Sp-12/Li-12.

> **NOTE: Sp-12 and Li-12 are close together so that a strike to either one usually catches the other. A strike to stomach (S-5), then to spleen (Sp-12) attacks yang and yin.**

(Continued)

TECHNIQUE # 43 (Continued)

From Pinan Yondan

BUNKAI

6. Place your left hand at the back of the attacker's head (left rear quadrant), and your right hand at his chin (right front quadrant).

7-9. Using two-way action, roll your opponent's head to your left, while turning around into a front stance, to throw him to the ground.

CAUTION: Use extreme care in practice. Do not jerk your partner's head, and do not hold on to him as he falls.

A-B In the close-up detail you can see how the defender does not actually grab the attacker's head, but instead controls with sticking pressure (muchimi).

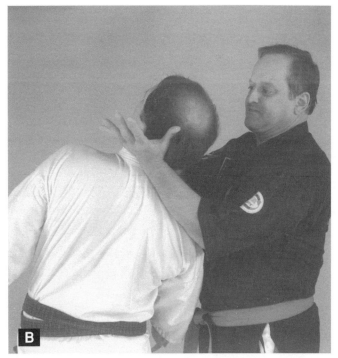

TECHNIQUE # 44
From Pinan Godan

1. Step forward into a left front stance, and thrust both fists forward and down, crossing the right over the left.

2. Draw your fists back toward your right armpit.

3-4. Open both hands and push them out, still crossed at the wrist, in front of your face.

(Continued)

TECHNIQUE # 44 (Continued)
From Pinan Godan

5-6. Roll your hands left over right, so that your right hand is palm up, closed into a fist, your left open hand lays palm down on top, and draw your hands to your right hip.

(Continued)

TECHNIQUE # 44 (Continued)
From Pinan Godan

BUNKAI

1. An assailant grabs your left wrist with his right hand.

2-3. Reach your right hand under your opponent's hand, hooking him on SI-6, to bend his wrist and lock his arm.

4. Draw your hands into your body to capitalize on your natural strength. This raises the attacker onto his toes, as it presses against SI-6.

> **NOTE: To secure the technique, flex your left wrist back, locking his wrist against your arms.**

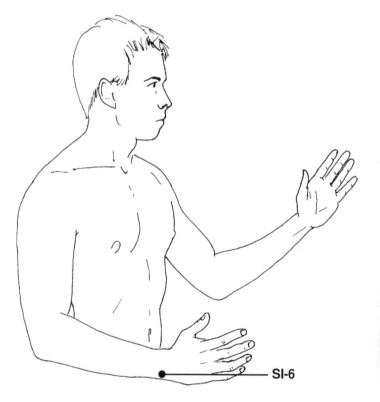

SI-6

3

(Continued)

TECHNIQUE # 44 (Continued)
From Pinan Godan

5. Roll your attacker's captured hand over, so his fingers point up and his palm faces you.

6-7. Apply a palm turn and take the assailant to the ground.

8. Follow-up with a strike to the base of the attacker's skull at B-10. (Do not strike in practice.)

> **NOTE: The sequence small intestine meridian to bladder meridian follows the diurnal cycle. Additional techniques beyond the movements of the kata itself are called "bunkai oyo" or "extended application."**

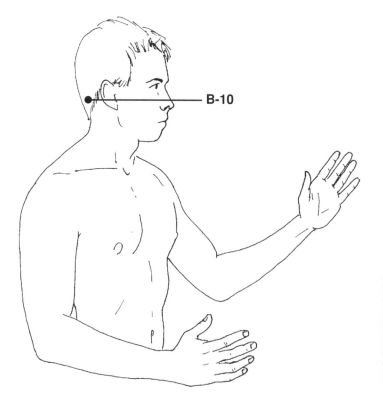

B-10

(Continued)

303

TECHNIQUE # 44 (Continued)
From Pinan Godan

A-F In close-up, the details of the tuité progression become clear.

[A-C] Locking on SI-6 causes the attacker's wrist to bend, trapping his hand between your crossed wrists, locking him at wrist and elbow. Note that the bend and rotation of his right hand places him in an inverted palm turn.

[D-F] The action of rolling his hand around to apply the final palm turn requires that you stick to it while you manipulate the joint (muchimi). The fact that you first locked his arm, lifting him up onto his toes, makes him helpless to resist as you change to the second lock, which applies pressure downward.

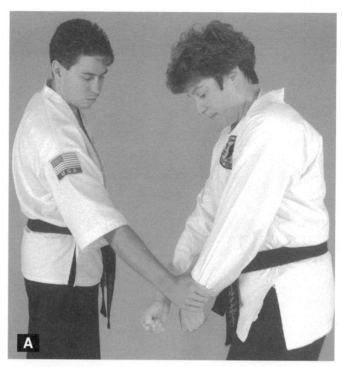

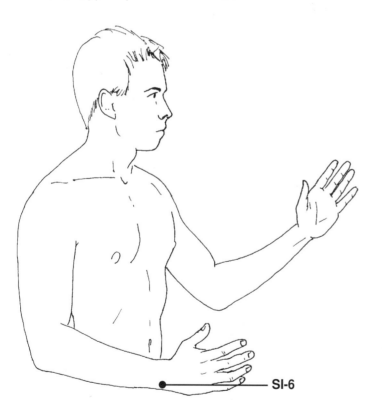

SI-6

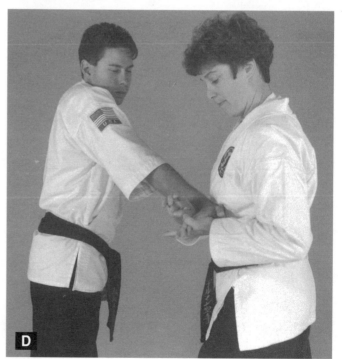

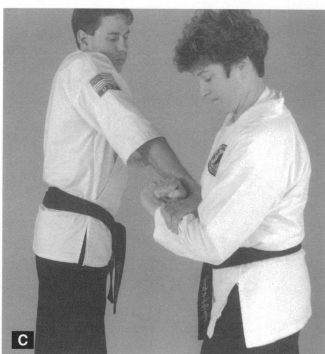

TECHNIQUE # 45
From Pinan Godan

1-3. From a left cat stance, step with your right foot, turning to your left and dropping into a kneeling stance, as you drive your hands downward, crossed at the wrists.

(Continued)

TECHNIQUE # 45 (Continued)
From Pinan Godan

BUNKAI

1-2. As an assailant attacks with a right punch, stick to his arm with your left wrist (muchimi), and guide it past your face.

3. Grab his wrist with your left hand, locking your fingers on H-6 and your thumb on SI-6. With your right hand, press against the back of the opponent's fist at TW-3, to apply a basic wrist reversal.

4. Turn to your left and begin to step in that direction with your right foot.

> **NOTE: With his wrist bent back, the turn of your body puts a strong outward rotation against the joint, creating complex torque.**

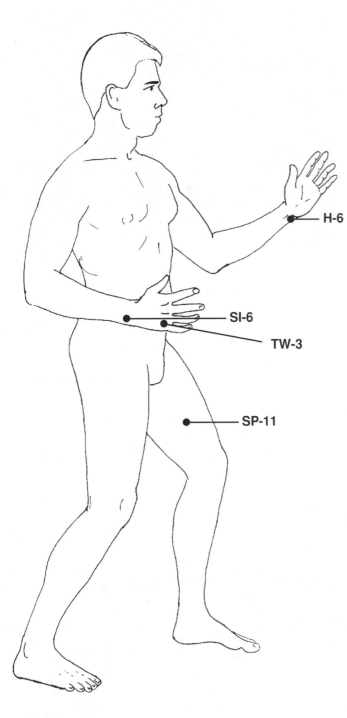

(Continued)

309

TECHNIQUE # 45 (Continued)

From Pinan Godan

BUNKAI

5-6. As you continue the step with your right leg, use your knee to attack Sp-11 on the inner thigh of the attacker's right leg.

Attacking Sp-11 further weakens H-6 because of the diurnal cycle of ki which flows from the spleen meridian to the heart meridian.

7-9. Drop to a kneeling posture, with all your weight falling on the attacker's wrist, to throw him forcefully to the ground.

NOTE: Leaning your full body weight against an opponent's twisted wrist is an example of using mechanical advantage. Even if he is much bigger, his locked joint cannot support your weight. To enhance this technique, it is important that you strive to cross your arms just as in the kata. This means that you will be pulling his wrist toward you slightly with your left hand, while driving his hand away with your right. This creates a sharp and irresistible two-way action in the middle of technique.

The observant reader may notice that in photos 8 & 9 the defender is in a left kneeling stance, rather than the right kneeling stance shown in the kata movement. This was done for safety's sake during the photo shoot. It would have been too risky for the "defender" to drive through the "attacker's" leg at Sp-11 in order to step into a right kneeling stance as the kata actually intends. Therefore, the "defender" merely tapped Sp-11, then dropped straight down into a left stance.

TECHNIQUE # 46
From Kusanku

The history of Kusanku kata reaches back to 1761 and is named for the Chinese martial artist who brought the original form to Okinawa. In Japan this form is called Kosokun or Kanku.

1. Begin with your open hands together in front of your abdomen.

2-3. Raise your hands above your face.

(Continued)

313

TECHNIQUE # 46 (Continued)
From Kusanku

4-6. Separate your hands and describe a circle starting just above head level and ending as your hands meet in front of your abdomen.

7. Look to the left and perform a left knife hand counter (shuto uke). Then immediately look to the right and perform a right knife hand counter (not shown).

(Continued)

TECHNIQUE # 46 (Continued)
From Kusanku

BUNKAI

1. An assailant reaches toward you with both hands to grab or push.

2. Bring both of your hands up between his, deflecting his arms up and to the outside.

NOTE: You must perform this movement as he is approaching. Once he has made contact with your body, you will not be able to knock his arms outward.

3-4. Stick to his right arm (muchimi) with your left arm and circle it down as you bring both your hands in symmetrical downward arcs.

(Continued)

TECHNIQUE # 46 (Continued)
From Kusanku

BUNKAI

5-6. Guiding the attacker's right hand with your left, strike him on the wrist at H-6 with the extended knuckle of the middle finger of your right fist.

7-8. Grab his right hand with your left and jerk him sharply forward as you angle your body sideways to strike SI-17 under the point of his jaw with the edge of your right hand.

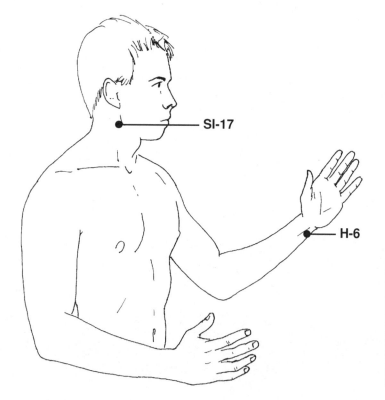

SI-17

H-6

> *NOTE: Attacking the heart meridian, followed by the small intestine meridian attacks yin and then yang.*
>
> *In the kata, the symmetrical movement of the hands followed by the left and right knife hand counters means that the first movement of the kata may be followed by either the right or left knife hand. We have illustrated this by showing the left knife hand in the solo movements, but using the right knife hand in application.*
>
> *In the kata movement it appears that the circling of the hands is against a frontal assault, and the knife hand counters are against attacks from the sides. Actually, the movements to the side mean that you must angle sideways to the opponent (as shown in the bunkai) to apply the technique properly.*

TECHNIQUE # 47
From Tomari-Bassai

The origins of Bassai (also pronounced Patsai) are unknown, but versions of this kata are widely practiced among Okinawan and Japanese styles (and Korean styles as well). These movements come from a version practiced in Ryukyu kempo Tomari-te.

1. Stand facing forward with your arms outstretched.

2. Cross your arms left over right in front of your body.

3. Looking to the left, strike out with your left fist and draw your right fist to your hip.

(Continued)

TECHNIQUE # 47 (Continued)
From Tomari-Bassai

BUNKAI

1. An assailant reaches toward you with both hands to grab or shove.

2-4. As the attacker approaches, press his arms across each other.

(Continued)

TECHNIQUE # 47 (Continued)
From Tomari-Bassai

BUNKAI

5-7. Trap the attacker's left hand between yours, and apply a basic palm turn to his right hand, thereby immobilizing both (see the detailed explanation below).

8-9. Angle sideways, and strike the attacker below the ear at TW-17 with your left fist.

NOTE: In this example, as before, a movement to the side means to angle sideways to the opponent, and not that the opponent approaches from the side.

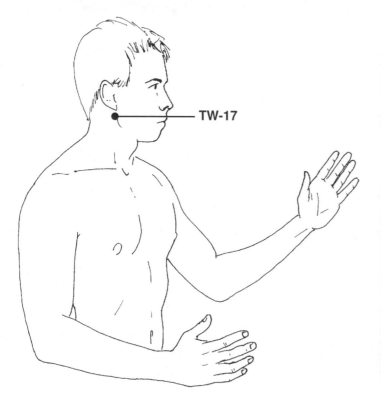

TW-17

7

(Continued)

TECHNIQUE # 47 (Continued)
From Tomari-Bassai

A-E In close-up it is easy to see the details of the tuité technique that immobilizes both of the attacker's hands.

[A-B] As you cross the attacker's arms, your left palm slips over the fingers of his right hand.

[C] Using the crook of your right wrist you control the attacker's wrist, drawing it toward you as you apply pressure on his fingers (two-way action).

[D-E] You apply pressure on the little finger side of the attacker's right hand with your palm (creating complex torque as you engage the palm turn) by pressing your elbow forward. This allows you to pin the assailant's left hand against your left forearm as you turn sideways (using body motion to increase the torque on the joint lock) and draw his trapped hands into your strength. This technique relies heavily on your skill at sticking (muchimi).

TECHNIQUE # 48
From Seiuchin

    Seiuchin is a kata of Chinese origin, and became popularized in Okinawan karate through Kanryo Higaonna (considered the founder of Naha-te) and his student Chojun Miyagi (founder of Goju-ryu).

1. Standing in a straddle stance with the toes pointed outward (this stance is called shiko-dachi), bring both open hands up to head level, touching back to back.

2-4. Squeeze both hands into fists and sweep them out to the sides.

(Continued)

TECHNIQUE # 48 (Continued)
From Seiuchin

BUNKAI

> **NOTE: This is a compound lock, a forearm turn applied against his left hand, and a head turn. Please exercise caution when executing the head turn.**

1. An assailant grabs you by the wrists.

2. In a rapid movement, swing your hands into your center (where you are strongest), turning them palm up, your left hand crossing beneath your right hand.

3. Reach up from underneath with your left hand, grabbing your opponent's left hand on L-10 in the meat of the thumb, and peel his left hand from your right wrist.

4. Grab the attacker's hair with your freed right hand, digging your knuckles into B-8 and GB-18 on the top of his head.

5. Draw your attacker's left hand toward your left and circle his head to your right.

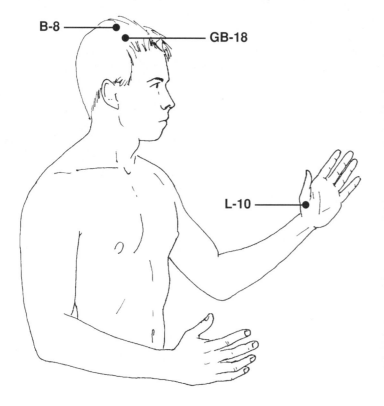

(Continued)

331

TECHNIQUE # 48 (Continued)

From Seiuchin

BUNKAI

6. Step out with your right foot into a straddle stance.

7-8. Sweep the attacker down in a circular motion, dropping his body against the point of your right knee.

WARNING: Use utmost restraint when practicing this technique. Do not jerk your partner's head or slam his back against your knee.

NOTE: The straddle stance is particularly well-suited for this application.

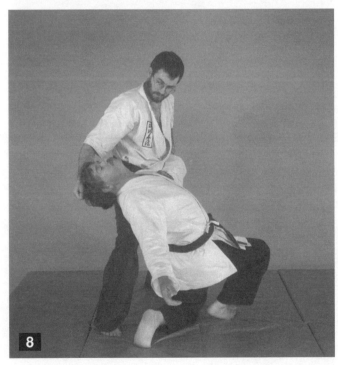

TECHNIQUE # 49
From Seiuchin

This sequence is from the version of Seiuchin taught by Tatsuo Shimabuku, who was a student of Chojun Miyagi.

1. In a left cat stance strike with a left forward elbow.

2. Shift your weight forward and punch downward with your right fist.

3-4. Step forward with your right foot and circle your left open hand outward, while drawing your right hand up close to your body. Continuing the motion of your hands, strike out with a right downward back fist, while drawing your left hand close to your body.

(Continued)

335

TECHNIQUE # 49 (Continued)
From Seiuchin

BUNKAI

1. An assailant seizes your lapel with his left hand.

2-4. Assume a left cat stance, grab the attacker's fist on the little finger side with your left hand, pressing on H-8, and in the same motion, strike his biceps at P-2 with your elbow.

> **NOTE: Your forward leg in the cat stance functions to protect your lower body from attack.**

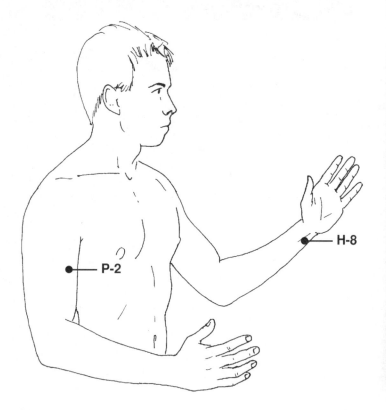

(Continued)

TECHNIQUE # 49 (Continued)
From Seiuchin

BUNKAI

5-6. Shift your weight forward and punch the bottom of the attacker's rib cage at Li-13.

7. Peel your attacker's hand — loosened by the preceding strikes — from your lapel and turn it so that the little finger side of his hand is up, applying a basic wrist turn/press.

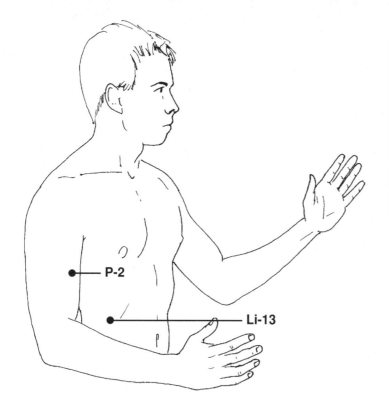

NOTE: This is a redundant application since either the elbow to P-2 or the punch to Li-13 will loosen the attacker's grip, and could end the fight altogether.

P-2

Li-13

(Continued)

TECHNIQUE # 49 (Continued)
From Seiuchin

BUNKAI

8-11. Step forward, pressing the attacker's hand close to his body so that his elbow is bent, and drop your elbow down onto the top of his forearm at LI-10.

> **CAUTION: Be very careful in practice to avoid injury.**

12. Strike the attacker at the base of the skull at GB-20.

> **NOTE:** The sequence of attacks to pericardium, large intestine, and gall bladder follows the cycle of destruction (fire to metal to wood). Additionally, the strike to the liver meridian followed by gall bladder is a yin/yang combination.

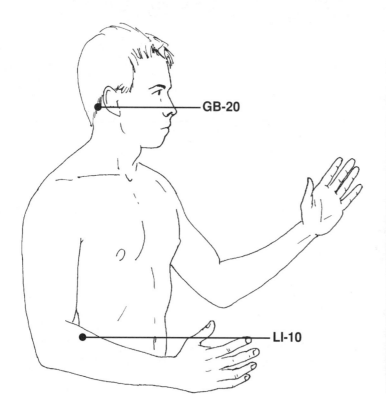

TECHNIQUE # 50
From Chinto

The origins of Chinto kata are lost to history. However, the kata is widely practiced and valued for its varied techniques and thorough integration of hand and foot maneuvers.

1-3. Standing in a straddle stance, extend your arms out to the sides, then bend your elbows swinging your fists inward to your chest.

(Continued)

TECHNIQUE # 50 (Continued)

From Chinto

4-5. Step your right foot behind your left to assume a cross-legged stance and execute a right downward counter (gedan barrai uke).

6. Perform a right front kick.

(Continued)

TECHNIQUE # 50 (Continued)
From Chinto

BUNKAI

1. Attacker's have grabbed your arms from each side.

2-4. Bring your arms up, outside the attackers' arms, trapping their hands in the crook of your elbows.

(Continued)

TECHNIQUE # 50 (Continued)
From Chinto

BUNKAI

5-6. Draw your fists to your chest, locking your attackers in simultaneous palm turns, and causing them to collide heads.

7-8. With your right hand, punch the attacker on your left under the ear at TW-17.

9. Knock the arm of the attacker on your right to the side (which turns his body toward you) and kick him square in the chest at Co-17.

CAUTION: A blow to Co-17 affects the heart. Do not actually strike this point in practice. However, in self-defense, an attack by multiple assailants represents a serious threat necessitating a serious response.

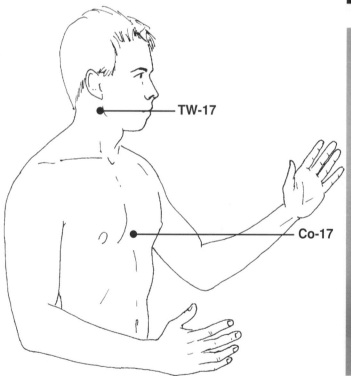

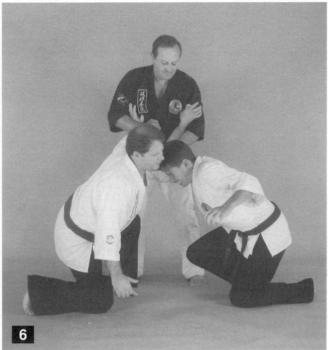

(Continued)

Greg Dillon of Indiana uses Tuité (grappling) and Kyusho-Jitsu (kick strike) against several opponents.

CONCLUSION

Today people are looking for quick fixes and easy, instant solutions. Tuité can seem to be such a quick fix. After all, it is a form of instant self-defense and its methods are easy to execute. However, it is not so easy to learn, nor is it learned instantly. Tuité-jitsu requires skill and sensitivity. These are acquired by thoughtful practice, with careful attention paid to the application of the underlying principles. However, with proper training it is possible to execute the tuité self-defense techniques gracefully, effortlessly and with great effect.

We recommend that you practice the techniques in this book many times, beginning very slowly. As they become more familiar, you can increase the speed and intensity of your training. However, always take care to practice in a safe and restrained manner.

Once you have mastered these movements, develop your own responses to various attacks. But, be careful to apply the principles of tuité at all times, so that your own techniques will be 100% effective.

APPENDIX:
POINT ATTACKING HAND CONFIGURATIONS

Because pressure points are discreet targets, martial artists have developed special hand configurations for attacking them. These hand positions are found throughout martial arts training, particularly in kata. However, the proper use of these formations is rarely explained or practiced.

KNUCKLE OF THE THUMB

The knuckle of the thumb is used to attack points which must be struck at an angle (such as GB-20). [Fig. 4]

BOTTOM FIST

The bottom surface of the fist, especially close to the wrist, is used to hammer hard surfaces (such as the skull). [Fig. 5]

FIST

The most basic striking surface is the first two knuckles of the clenched fist. This is typically used to attack points on large body surfaces, such as the abdomen. [Fig. 1]

FOREKNUCKLES

The flat of the fingers, the surface used to knock on a door, is used to attack points on hard bony regions, such as the back of the hand. This hand configuration is commonly applied against the elbow at TW-11. [Fig. 2]

BASE OF THE THUMB

The first metacarpal, the bone at the base of the thumb, is used especially to attack pressure points on the wrist. [Fig. 3]

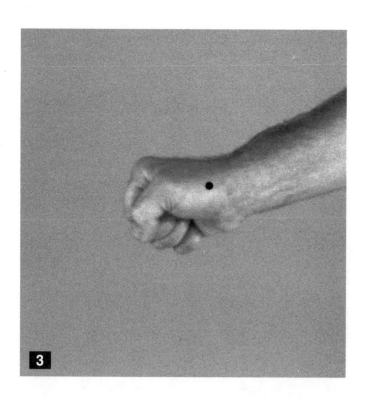

3

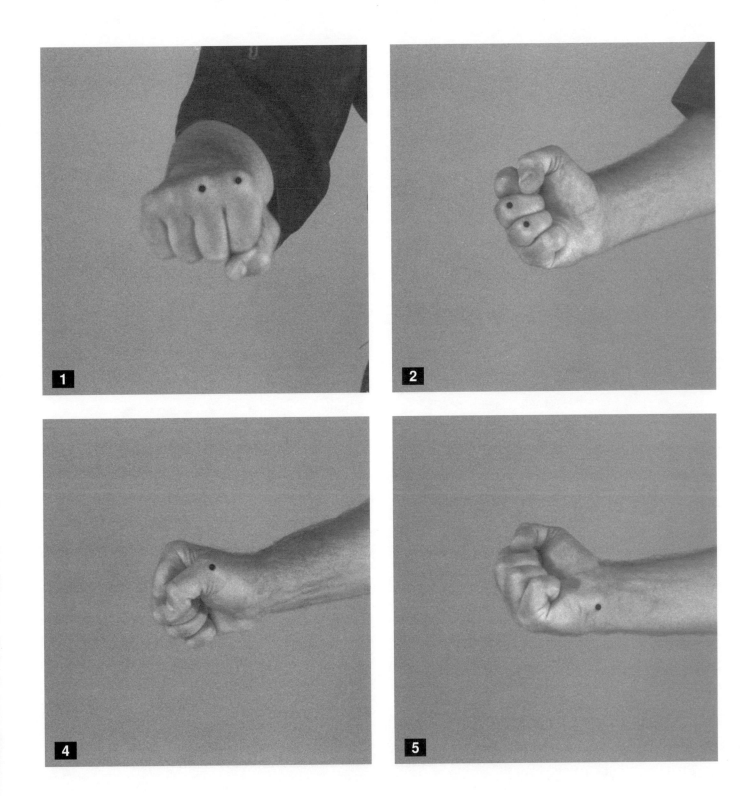

(Continued)

SMALL KNUCKLE

The knuckle of the little finger is not very strong, yet it is extremely useful to attack pressure points on the arm (such as LI-10). [Fig. 6]

SINGLE KNUCKLE (INDEX FINGER)

By extending the second knuckle of the index finger, a penetrating, arrow-like fist is formed. This fist is particularly suited to attack points with downward energy (such as S-7, at the hinge of the jaw). [Fig. 7]

SINGLE KNUCKLE (MIDDLE FINGER)

By extending the second knuckle of the middle finger the fist becomes like the head of a spear. Use this fist to strike upward (for example, to SI-18). [Fig. 8]

CHICKEN BEAK

Squeeze the ends of all five digits tightly together to strike with the fingertips. This shape allows one to reach around to attack points at hard to reach angles (such as TW-17). The action of striking with this hand configuration resembles the pecking motion of a chicken, thus the name. [Fig. 9]

BENT WRIST

When the hand is tightly bent forward (palmar flexion) the back of the wrist (dorsal surface) forms a hard striking surface. It is mostly used to strike from underneath, such as striking up under the arm at H-2. [Fig. 10]

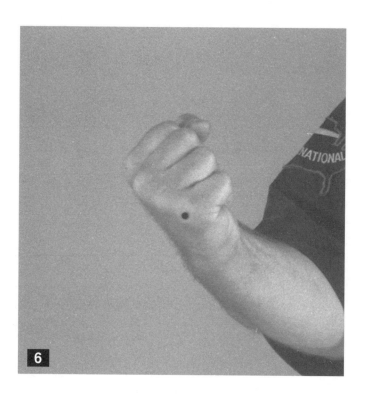

6

NOTE: Placement of thumb to lock these hand positions into place.

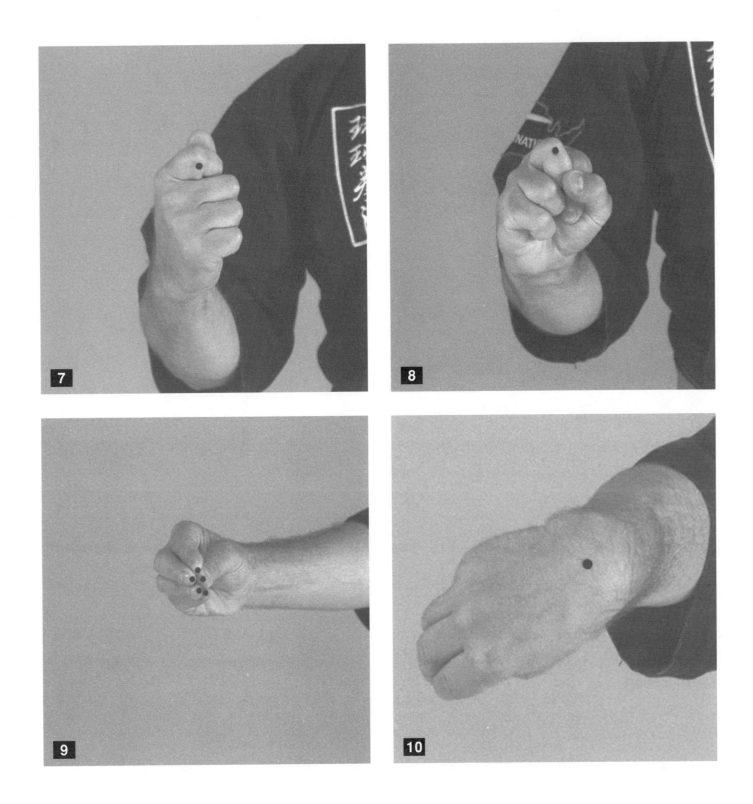

(Continued)

YANG PALM

When the hand is bent strongly back (dorsiflexion) the heel of the palm forms a hard surface. This is used to attack yin meridians, or yin body surfaces, those which are soft and somewhat yielding such as the torso. [Fig. 11]

> **NOTE: This technique hand is usually delivered with a twisting action.**

YIN PALM

The yin palm is used to attack yang meridians or yang surfaces (such as the skull). The hand configuration yields and conforms to the target being hit. Vital energy (ki) is "pooled" in the center of the palm and transferred into the target. [Fig. 12]

KNIFE EDGE

With the fingers straight, and the hand slightly cupped, the edge of the hand (along the fifth metacarpal) becomes an effective tool. It is especially used to strike the neck, because the line of the hand fits into the front edge of the neck muscle (the anterior margin of the sternocleidomastoid) where three important knock-out points (S-10, S-9, SI-17) are located. [Fig. 13]

CUPPED HAND

With the back of the hand rounded, a slapping strike of the cupped hand connects at two distinct points. The points of impact are the knuckle of the thumb and the base of the little finger. [Fig. 14]

RIDGE HAND

The side edge of the open hand is used to strike two points in close proximity. The two distinct striking surfaces are the knuckle of the thumb and the base of index finger. [Fig. 15]

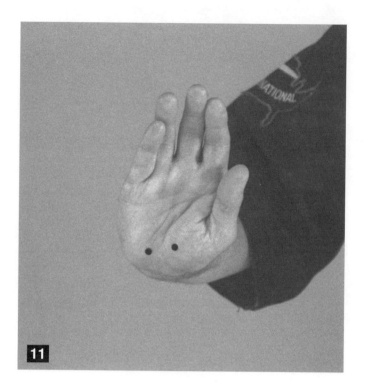

11

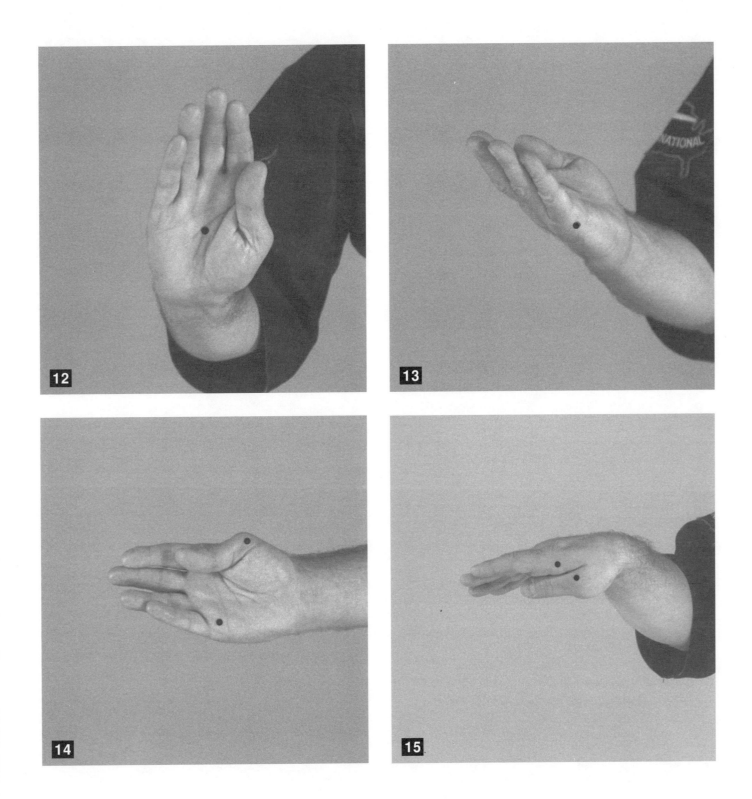

(Continued)

It is important to understand that hand configurations such as the "ridge hand" actually strike two points at once. Pressure points S-9 and S-10 on the neck are oriented exactly matching the striking surfaces of the ridge hand. For this reason, a light blow with the ridge hand produces unconsciousness.

A. S-9 and S-10 are located to the side of the throat.

B. The striking surfaces of the ridge hand and these two points match up perfectly.

C. Notice that as the blow is delivered (from about one inch away) the hand looks still, but the recipient is falling as if hit with a baseball bat.

D-F. The "victim" is knocked out cold, and must be revived using energy restoration methods. Without proper revival to restore the balance of ki, a pressure point knock out can result in illness. For this reason, **NEVER KNOCK OUT ANYONE SIMPLY TO SEE IF IT WILL WORK!!!** Train under a qualified instructor and learn the proper techniques to restore energy.

CAUTION: This example is to illustrate how effortless — and serious — pressure point techniques can be. DO NOT ATTEMPT THIS!

NOTE: Energy restoration techniques are covered in KYUSHO-JITSU: The Dillman Method of Pressure Point Fighting, pages 91-101, and in DILLMAN PRESSURE POINT VIDEO # 5: Healing and Energy Restoration.

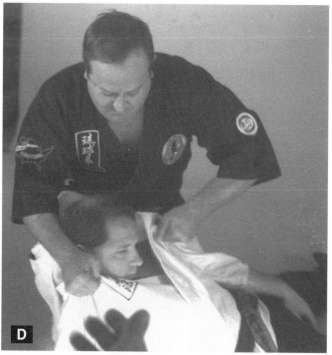

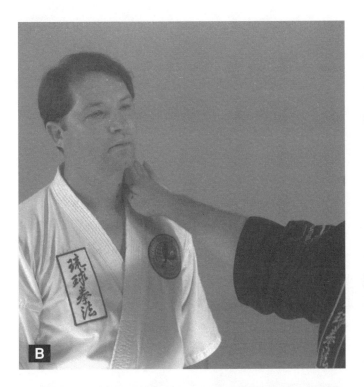

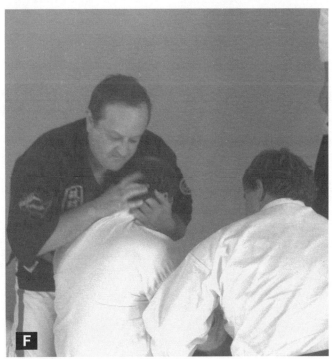

George A. Dillman, Jr. does a pressure point arm technique — Tuité — to drop his brother Allen B. Dillman. (Feb. 1993 photo: by Kim Dillman)